Writing Power

Engaging Thinking Through Writing

Adrienne Gear

Stenhouse Publishers
PORTLAND, MAINE

Pembroke Publishers Limited
MARKHAM, ONTARIO

DEDICATION

In loving memory of my dear mum,
Sheila Gear,
who gifted the world with stories
and goodness

© 2011 Pembroke Publishers
538 Hood Road
Markham, Ontario, Canada L3R 3K9
www.pembrokepublishers.com

Published in the U.S. by Stenhouse Publishers
480 Congress Street
Portland, ME 04101
www.stenhouse.com

"Invitation" by Shel Silverstein in margin on page 31: COPYRIGHT © 1974, renewed
2002 EVIL EYE MUSIC, LLC. Reprinted with permission from the Estate of Shel Silverstein and HarperCollins Children's Books.

Every effort has been made to contact copyright holders for permission to reproduce
borrowed material. The publishers apologize for any such omissions and will be pleased
to rectify them in subsequent reprints of the book.

We acknowledge the financial support of the Government of Canada through the Book
Publishing Industry Development Program (BPIDP) for our publishing activities.

We acknowledge the assistance of the Government of Ontario through the Ontario
Media Development Corporation's Ontario Book Initiative.

Library and Archives Canada Cataloguing in Publication

Gear, Adrienne
    Writing power : teaching writing strategies that engage thinking / Adrienne Gear.

Includes bibliographical references and index.
Issued also in electronic format.
ISBN 978-1-55138-263-0

    1. Composition (Language arts)—Study and teaching (Elementary). 2. Written
communication—Study and teaching (Elementary). I. Title.

LB1576.G43 2011   372.62'3044   C2011-904782-9

eBook format ISBN 978-1-55138-827-4

Editor: Kat Mototsune
Cover Design: John Zehethofer
Typesetting: Jay Tee Graphics Ltd.

Printed and bound in Canada
9 8 7 6 5 4 3 2 1

MIX
Paper from
responsible sources
FSC® C004071

Contents

Preface

Every January 25, my family and invited guests would gather around the dining room table for a special supper to honor the late poet Robert Burns. My sisters, mum and I, and of course my dad would all be dressed in traditional tartan kilts. With bagpipe music blaring, my sisters and I would march into the living room, carrying in the haggis on a silver platter. With much pomp and circumstance my dad would toast the haggis, stab it with his long silver sword, and recite a traditional Robert Burns grace: "Some hae meat and canna eat/And some wad eat that want it/But we hae meat, and we can eat/Sae let the Lord be thankit." After supper, my dad would rise from his chair and read aloud some of his favorite Robbie Burns poems. We sat, listened, and watched as he read those words we'd all come to know so well. Even though he had recited the words of his beloved Scottish poet many times, my dad would often be moved to tears.

My late father was a passionate man, but perhaps his deepest passion was for the English language. Simply put, he was in love with words; moved by the power of a poem; fascinated by the structure of a sonnet. He visibly demonstrated every time he read aloud the works of Burns, Shakespeare, or Whitman how deeply the words of a writer could affect the reader. At the time, I did not realize how important a lesson that was, nor how significant an impact this reciprocal and intimate link between writer and reader would have on me or on this book. Of all the many gifts my father gave me, it is his deep appreciation and passion for words for which I am most grateful.

Strongly influenced by my father, I have always been a word collector. I started collecting quotes, words, and poems as a teenager and recorded them in various Quote Collection notebooks over the years. Sometimes they would be written in fancy calligraphy and accompanied by illustrations; other times, simply scribbled onto the corner of a page. I think I watched the movie *Dead Poets Society* more than twenty times, scribbling the words of the poems that the Robin Williams character, John Keating, read out to his students. I have read, reread, and memorized these quotes over the years; written them in birthday and sympathy cards; read them out on special occasions. These collections of words written by others have often been of great comfort to me, brought me solace and joy, laughter and tears—I consider them to be precious gifts. Words, I have come to understand, are indeed gifts, bringing with them far more than the ink on a page, but an invitation to think, to question, to connect, to visualize, to reanalyze and rethink our lives, our relationships, and our world. I have always considered myself to be a reader—however, up until now I never realized how strong a connection the writer and the reader have with one another. Without the writer, there would be no reader. Without the reader, it can be argued, there would be no writer.

The intimate relationship between reader and writer is the underlying foundation of this book. While many professional books on writing instruction focus on the process of writing, I wanted this book to do more than that. My goal for writing this book is to not only help our students better understand *how* to write or *what* to write, but also to let them see *why* we write. I want them to come to understand that there is more to writing than what is constructed on the page— it's also how that construction of words affects and influences whoever happens to be on the receiving end of them. Teaching writing should address this relationship between writer and reader.

I know it's time to write when my brain becomes too heavy to hold all my thinking, and thankfully I let writing lighten the load. My brain has been heavily weighted with thinking about Writing Power since I had a revelation while sitting in my living room surrounded by piles of picture books. It was at that moment that I realized that Reading Power could be also viewed from the flip side—from the side of the writer rather than the reader. And out of that "ah-ha" moment comes this question: Can awareness of our readers' thinking affect and enhance our ability to write? I still don't know the answer to this question, but this book may be the first step toward discovering one. Ralph Fletcher states, "Alas, there is no miracle for growing young writers" (Fletcher, 2006). Perhaps developing an awareness of the minds and hearts of the readers we write for may be, at the very least, the beginning of "growing" better writers.

Adrienne Gear

Introduction

When I was in elementary school, writing consisted of one double period on Thursday afternoon referred to as "creative writing." In this double period we all wrote on the same topic: "My Summer," "Pets," "Halloween," "My Friend," etc. "Creative writing" did not include instruction from the teacher on any aspects of the craft of writing, nor were we read a carefully selected picture book that reflected a particular trait we would then try to integrate into our own writing. No planning, brainstorming, or pre-writing took place. One could say that, once a week, we were given a topic and then asked to do what would, by today's standards, be considered a "cold write." At the end of the double period, a few of us would be selected to read aloud our quietly crafted pieces of writing. Then papers would be handed in and the red pen of the teacher would scratch, circle, underline, and highlight all the spelling, punctuation, and grammar mistakes. These mistakes were counted and would be the only factor in determining our grade. No editing was done. No consideration of style, voice, or word choice was given. Corrections were done and "good copies" were completed the next week.

Thankfully, we have come a long way since then. Thanks to the generous insight into the gift of writing and writing instruction from such fine educators as Donald Murray, Donald Graves, Lucy Calkins, Georgia Heard, Shelley Harwayne, Ralph Fletcher, Joann Portalupi, and Ruth Culham—to name a few—writing is now considered a process rather than a product; writers are encouraged to draw from their own lives and experiences as sources of writing; literature is often used as a model for good writing; and, in terms of assessment and evaluation, value is placed as much on meaning, word choice, and ideas as on mechanics.

Connecting Reading Power and Writing Power

While writing has always been a personal hobby, my passion has always been reading. My work over the past ten years has focused primarily on guiding teachers to find ways to enhance their reading instruction to include specific and explicit instruction in comprehension strategies. Developing the Reading Power teaching practice was a way of taking a practical approach to a complex problem—helping our students become not just better readers of text, but also better thinkers of text. The shift from assigning and assessing comprehension questions to providing purposeful and explicit instruction in comprehension strategies has been a significant one that we might equate to the "big shift" that occurred in how we provide writing instruction.

It is both a blessing and a curse to be in a constant state of reflection. While I join the many thousands of teachers who revel in their comfort zone when it comes time to pull out a unit that I've taught 17 times before, Reading Power would never have evolved had I not reflected on the fact that there were some serious gaps in my reading instruction. In fact, there was more than just a gap—I can say now, looking back, that my reading instruction was nonexistent. While no one would question the fact that I "did" reading with my students, I did little to teach reading. Recognizing that reading instruction should not end once students have acquired the ability to decode and that all teachers are responsible for providing explicit instruction in reading, no matter what grade they teach, was a revelation for me. The result of that revelation was determining what reading instruction, or more specifically comprehension instruction, might "look like."

Reading Power was considered somewhat of a breakthrough for many teachers because it was new. There had been little in the way of comprehension instruction being implemented in many classrooms. Primary teachers focused their reading instruction on phonemic awareness, while intermediate teachers, for the most part, provided opportunities for their students to apply reading skills to projects, novel studies, and reading-response activities; however, explicit instruction in reading comprehension was rare. *Reading Power* provided teachers with a practical way into comprehension instruction.

Writing instruction, on the other hand, has already experienced many breakthroughs in the past 20 years. So much has been explored on the subject of teaching writing that one might now feel there is almost too much to choose from. The "big shift" that happened with reading comprehension in the last ten years occurred in the field of writing more than 30 years ago. Donald Graves' research and revolutionary approach to writing instruction, known as the Writing Process, changed the face of writing instruction throughout North America and the world (Graves, 1975). Prior to this, writing in schools consisted of the "creative writing" classes I remember. Little or no writing instruction went into those writing periods, other than a strong emphasis on conventions and spelling. Donald Graves and his contemporaries, including Lucy Calkins and Ralph Fletcher, introduced us to a whole new world of writing as a process that included planning, drafting, editing, mini-lessons, conferencing, and nudging children to go deeper with a word or a thought, to use their own experiences and observations to write about. Writing instruction in schools was never the same.

The Traits of Writing (Hicks & Spandel, 1997) and/or 6+1 Traits (Culham, 2003) represent another significant breakthrough in writing instruction and assessment. This concept also changed the way teachers provide writing instruction by showing a system designed to teach students the craft of quality writing. Breaking down good writing into very specific traits, such as voice, organization, ideas, and conventions, has proven to be very effective in providing quality writing instruction and improving writing skills. The Write Traits model has been implemented throughout North America and, again, has changed the way teachers think about, plan, execute, and assess writing in their classrooms.

"The skill of writing is to create a context in which other people can think."
—Edwin Schlossberg

Both the writing process and the writing traits models have been instrumental in influencing the way teachers provide writing instruction in their classrooms. One could say that the writing process helped explain the *how* of writing—how to plan, draft, write, edit, etc.—and that the writing traits model helped explain the *what* of writing—what specific elements of good writing should be considered. But, as I do often when evaluating my teaching practice, I found myself thinking that something was missing. And what appeared to be missing was the *why* of writing.

Now this, I admit, feels like venturing into some uncharted territory. I acknowledge with gratitude the many professional resources already available that provide theory, insight, and ideas into providing effective writing instruction for our young writers. And while there are vast amounts of research, theory, and practice on enhancing writing instruction through process and through insight into what good writing includes, despite my valiant effort I was not able to uncover any research or practice on how awareness of the readers' thinking might help to guide and perhaps enhance one's ability to write.

It is not my intent, in writing this book, to replicate or repeat the wealth of expertise that has come before me. The Writing Process and the Writing Traits are just two of many successful methods many of us have used and will continue to implement in our writing program. Just as Reading Power was never intended as a replacement for, but rather as an addition to, current reading instruction, so too is Writing Power intended to enhance your current writing instruction, not to replace the things that are already working for you. It is, however, intended to help teachers introduce their young writers to the importance of developing an awareness of their audience and to write with the intent of inviting their reader into the text via a consideration of our thinking brains. It is the goal of Writing Power to move beyond the "how to write" toward the "why we write," and to introduce writers to the important, yet often forgotten, aspect of writing: the reader.

What to Expect

This book is designed to help teachers develop an effective writing program. The feedback I receive from teachers about my *Reading Power* books is that they appreciate how practical they are and how easily they can follow the lessons. I have tried to do the same with this book, providing clearly outlined, often scripted, lessons. As I believe it is important for teachers to model writing with their students, I have also tried to provide examples to use for modeling at those moments when our writing brain goes blank because we are focused on the fact that Emma is poking Henry in the ribs with her scissors! I have also included many reproducible organizers to accompany the lessons—because teachers *love* these easy-to-use tools, and so do I!

The book is divided into three sections.

- Writing for the Reader begins, like *Reading Power*, by describing some important background information in both reading and writing theory and research. This gives you the background to understand where Writing Power came from and how it is linked to Reading Power. This section includes a chapter on the Writing Power lesson framework, with my thoughts and ideas about writer's notebooks, conferencing, and editing; it also discusses assessment and provides sample rubrics for various grade levels to use when evaluating students' writing.
- The next section of the book introduces the "big picture" lessons that cover the basics of writing and introduce some important writing concepts to students. The first chapter in this section introduces the term "alocognition"—the other side of a reader's metacognition—to refer to the purpose of writing and the concept of writers inviting their readers to think. The chapter on Thinking Power introduces students to the concept of Brain Pockets: where writers get their ideas for writing. Narrative Power is about the different writing structures that are focused on in this book. The Technical Power chapter provides

"A small drop of ink produces that which makes thousands think."
—Lord Byron

teachers with lessons for introducing a wide variety of writing techniques that, once introduced to students, are applied throughout the Writing Power lessons: these techniques include personification, voice, similes, and triple-scoop words. The intent is that students learn the techniques and then are given many opportunities to apply them in a variety of different writing pieces.

- Finally, the Writing Power Lessons section outlines explicit and sequential writing lessons that focus on one of the five comprehension strategies that many are familiar with: connect, question, visualize, infer, and transform. This time we approach the strategies from the perspective of the writer and look at ways that writing can engage our readers' thinking. These writing lessons follow a structured approach based on the writing process of planning, writing, conferencing, editing, and sharing. As in *Reading Power*, suggested anchor books (marked P for Primary and I for Intermediate) are recommended for each lesson. Teachers who already have *Reading Power* book collections will be able to use many of the same titles for these writing lessons.

It is important that I take a moment here to address one of the many issues I encountered when developing this book—trying to develop writing lessons that would meet the needs of every teacher of Grades 1 through 7. What was manageable about Reading Power was that it met the needs of many different reading and grade levels—students can still "think" even though they may not yet know how to read, and decoding is not a prerequisite of thinking. So Grade 1 and 2 students who are developing reading skills can still make a connection or visualize while the teacher reads. But writing is different. You can think even if you don't yet know how to read, but you can't write if you don't yet know how to print. The ability to print is a prerequisite of developing writing. Grade 1 teachers might take a look at some of these lessons and think *There is no way my kids could do that. They can't even print their names!* Early primary teachers will most likely not be ready to start teaching these writing lessons until the final term of the year because, up until that time, the students are learning how to hold their pencils, form letters, stretch out sounds, etc. But as you will see from the Grade 1 writing samples in this book, these students are capable of developing ideas effectively on paper as their printing skills improve.

It is not the intent of this book that every teacher of every grade teach every lesson to his or her class. Teachers need to adapt the lessons for their grade and ability level, and to give themselves permission to choose only the lessons that their students can manage. I do believe, however, that early primary teachers can begin to plant the seed of "writers engaging their readers" long before any of these lessons are taught. A comment such as "I really like the way this writer invited us all to make connections to this book" or "This writer really used words that helped me paint a picture in my mind" after a read-aloud is enough to get children to begin to think about the important relationship between reader and writer.

The "big picture" lessons are intended to be taught prior to and during the strategy lessons in the third section of the book.

Although anchor books are marked as P for Primary and I for Intermediate, the picture books can be used with both primary and intermediate students to model particular writing techniques and thinking strategies.

Writing for the Reader

Why do writers write? There are perhaps many individual answers to that question, but we can agree that most writers write because they have ideas they want to share with others—to make concrete an abstract thought; to make tangible an idea that, until the moment the pencil hit the paper, belonged only to the writer but soon will belong to everyone. Writers "gift" their readers with words in the hope of touching them in some way—through laughter or tears, questions, connections, visual images. Writers share pieces of themselves and the things they care about with their readers, reaching out to them with an unspoken invitation to think.

I asked myself: *If this is why writers write, why aren't we teaching this to our students?* Why isn't focusing on the *why* of writing at least a part of our writing instruction? If I already know that a reader is going to be thinking when they are reading my writing, why am I not making some adjustments to my writing in order to support their thinking?

This book was designed to promote the idea that writers and readers are intimately connected. It is my belief that this relationship needs to be acknowledged and reinforced every time students begin to write. I think that too often students are given the wrong impression of why we write; they think they are writing simply and solely because they have to hand something in. Writing to engage thinking can, in fact, help change our focus and purpose for writing in school, and can perhaps help students develop a greater sense of the reader–writer connection.

1   What Is Writing Power?

Theory and Practice in Writing and Reading Instruction

Research drives our practice. Whether we are aware of it or not, most of the teaching methods we use today are grounded in the results of research. While many studies play a role, there are a few pioneers in the field whose research has had a revolutionary impact on our teaching practice. In the field of writing instruction, we cannot deny the enormous influence of Donald Graves' research into the writing process and Robert Deiderich's research into the traits of writing. These researchers, among many, have played key roles in how instruction in both reading and writing has evolved in classrooms over the past 30 years.

The Writer's Workshop

The Writing Process: The *How* of Effective Writing

- Plan
- Draft
- Write
- Edit
- Rewrite
- Publish

In the 1980s, Donald Graves and his many mentors, supporters, and followers —including Donald Murray, Lucy Calkins, and Ralph Fletcher—introduced us to the notion of the writing process. Through Graves' research we learned that the process of writing can be broken down into specific stages, including planning, drafting, writing, and editing. These stages can be taught and integrated into a procedure called the Writer's Workshop. Graves' research into the process of writing resulted in writing workshops being created by teachers to guide students through planning, drafting, writing, conferencing, editing, sharing, and publishing. Gone were the days when "creative writing" was one hour on Thursday afternoons in which teachers assigned the weekly topics and where assessment was based primarily on conventions. In the writing workshop, students write daily and choose their own topics for writing; assessment is based more on the writer's craft than on how many spelling and grammatical errors there are. Teachers, through mini-lessons, provide explicit instruction in various techniques of writing that help move developing writers forward in their understanding and knowledge of the writing process.

The Write Traits (6+1 Traits of Writing)

The Six Writing Traits: The *What* of Effective Writing

- Ideas
- Organization
- Voice
- Word Choice
- Sentence Fluency
- Conventions

The Write Traits framework derived from the 1960s research of Paul B. Diederich. He was curious to know whether people could agree on what makes writing work and whether they could come up with a language to describe what they found. Diederich determined that the five elements most valued in writing were ideas, mechanics, form, wording, and flavor. In 1984, his work was used by a group of teachers from Oregon, lead by Vicki Spandel and Jeff Hicks, who worked with the Northwest Regional Educational Laboratory (NWREL) to redefine the criteria. This resulted in the now widely known criteria for good writing that is commonly referred to as the Six Traits (Spandel, 2001). Ruth Culham later took this framework and added a seventh trait (publishing), which resulted in the 6+1 Traits of Writing. Defining these traits, developing a language for what good writers do, and creating assessment rubrics for teachers has resulted in improved writing instruction by helping teachers set goals and standards for students, and by providing a set of common expectations for good writers.

Reading Comprehension and Reading Power

The Writer's Workshop and the Writing Traits, both results of significant research, have redefined in the last 20 years how teachers teach writing. Through both approaches, teachers have been given the tools and the language to provide more effective writing instruction. Similarly, David Pearson's research in the 1980s into what proficient readers do has changed the way we think about and provide reading instruction. No longer is reading comprehension about assigning ten questions to answer at the end of the chapter; rather, it is about teaching students specific thinking strategies that enable them to interact with the text to enhance understanding. Once again, the results of research have enabled teachers to create a common framework and a common language for reading comprehension instruction.

I developed Reading Power ten years ago as a practical way for the teachers at my school to teach these comprehension strategies to students. This metacognitive approach to reading focuses on five specific comprehension strategies—connect, question, visualize, infer, and transform (synthesize)—and helps students to develop an awareness of thinking while they read. Reading is not about just what is going on in the book, but also about what is going on in the reader's head. Thanks to David Pearson's research, comprehension is no longer considered something you "do" with your students, but is instead something you teach your students. Comprehension instruction was the missing piece of many reading programs across the country.

Proficient readers are able to
- Make Connections
- Ask Questions
- Visualize
- Draw Inferences
- Determine Importance
- Analyze and Synthesize Text
- Monitor Comprehension

From Reading to Writing

Looking back, I believe that Writing Power evolved as a result of my strong connection to children's literature. Literature has always been an integral part of my teaching practice. Not only has using picture books, novels, and nonfiction texts as anchors for my teaching become common practice for me, but my students also have come to expect that a book will be the starting point for most lessons I teach. For those of you familiar with Reading Power, you will know that picture books play a significant role in the teaching and supporting of the Reading Power strategies to your students. I have developed many Reading Power booklists with suggested titles for teachers to use when teaching and practicing the different strategies.

Reading through hundreds of books and organizing them around strategies brings me a joy that is almost indescribable. I live for a new book, a new title, a new release. People may think I'm crazy to spend so much time reading picture books into the wee hours of the night and trying to decide which strategy each might best support. "How do you have time?" they ask. Time stands still when I am sitting with of a pile of new books spread out in front of me. When I open a new book, I can feel my heart begin to speed up. I'm eager with anticipation to discover the treasures that lie beneath the cover. I love to savor the words, drink

"The more you read, the more you will write. The better the stuff you read, the better the stuff you will write."
—Annie Dillard

in the pictures, and allow myself to feel, to laugh, to cry, to be moved, to think. I love the feel of the pages in my hands and I even love the smell of unread pages. I have always considered the words of others as a gift to me. Sometimes it is a gift that I decide to return, but other times it is a gift to treasure, to read over and over, to keep under my pillow until it's old and worn, because it's just that good.

One day, while I was sitting in front of yet another pile of new picture books and sorting them into strategy piles, a thought suddenly occurred to me. Why is it that I find sorting these books into the different reading strategies so easy now? I can pick up any book, read through it, and within seconds determine if it's a Connect book or a Question book. How is that possible? One might believe it's because I've had so much practice. I might respond that it's because I'm so clever! But, looking closer, the answer would appear to have nothing to do with me. And as much as I would like to take credit for being so experienced and clever, I must acknowledge that the reason it is easy has nothing to do with me and everything to do with the writing. The writing itself invited my thinking, invited me to question, to connect, to visualize, or to infer. And suddenly, in that instant, I saw Reading Power from the other side—from the writing side.

We've spent the last several years focusing our students on what good readers do when they read. But let's stop for a moment and ask ourselves why this is possible. Why do we make connections to some books but not so much to others? Why do we ask questions readily when reading this text but not that one? How are we able to visualize more easily with particular books? Answer: Because the writing invites us to do so.

Good writing naturally results in readers making connections, asking questions, drawing inferences, visualizing, and transforming their thinking in some way. But are all writers aware of these strategies and able to have them in mind when they construct their text? Could this awareness influence how they write? How do writers go about ensuring that their writing engages readers? Is it technique? Topic? These are just some of the questions that resulted in Writing Power. And just as thinking is the underlying principal of Reading Power, so too is thinking the focus of Writing Power. But instead of asking writers to think about their writing, Writing Power is about writers thinking about their readers. Thinking is the link between reading and writing. When we read, we have one eye on the page and the other inside our heads, searching for ways to interact with the text and deepen our understanding. When we write, we have one eye on the page and the other on our reader, searching for ways to ensure that those interactions to take place.

So what is Writing Power? It is an approach to writing instruction that

- is structured
- adds a layer of thinking to writing
- is a way of linking reading instruction with writing instruction
- emphasizes the process and techniques of writing rather than the product
- focuses on the *why* of writing, rather than just the *what* and *how*
- does not replace writing workshops or the writing traits, but integrates them
- provides topics, anchor books, and instruction to support writing

Teachers who are already implementing Reading Power strategies in their classrooms can easily link reading and writing by focusing on the same strategy in both reading and writing lessons. For example, at the beginning of the school year, if the reading strategy you are focusing on is making connections, then your writing lessons can focus on inviting readers to make connections.

2   The Components of Writing Power

One of the challenges I experienced when first integrating the writing workshop into my classroom many years ago was the time it took. Allowing large blocks of time for writing every day was not always easy to do. Another challenge for me was the unstructured manner in which the writing workshop evolved. I had students at all stages of the writing process writing about all different things at all different times. Somebody was conferencing with a buddy in this corner; somebody was planning his or her next story in that corner; someone was drafting a story in another corner. This was a good thing in theory, but a bit of a nightmare in terms of management.

For these reasons, I have taken a more structured approach to Writing Power. While students are still writing from their own experiences, they are all focusing on the same writing topic and same writing technique each week. They follow an adapted writing process in which everyone plans, writes, edits, conferences, and shares at the same time.

Writing Power Lesson Framework

The Writing Power process, adapted from Donald Graves, looks like this:

1. Find and organize your idea(s)
2. Write (sometimes trying a new writing technique)
3. Conference with a partner and edit
4. Share and publish (sometimes!)

The lessons in this book follow a structured framework and are organized around a weekly schedule of three or four writing blocks per week. These blocks can run anywhere from 30 to 45 minutes, depending on your time table and grade level. Each week a new writing topic is introduced: this topic is the focus for all four lessons during that week.

Lesson 1: Topic and Planning (Teacher Directed/Independent)

Strategy Focus: Each lesson begins with a reminder to students about the strategy they will be focusing on in their writing. Ideally, it is the same strategy you are focusing on in reading:

> Good readers make connections when they read. As writers, our goal today is to write something that will invite our readers to make connections.

Lesson Focus: Each lesson focuses on a specific topic that lends itself well to the strategy focus: e.g., connecting to friends; visualizing weather.

Teachers following these lesson guidelines on a weekly basis can use the Writing Power Weekly Planning sheet on page 22 as a way of planning and tracking their topics, strategies, anchor books, student conferences, and student sharing.

The following phrases can be used by primary teachers to describe the lessons in the Writing Power framework:

Lesson 1: Time to Plan, Stan!
Lesson 2: Time to Write, Zyke!
Lesson 3: Time to Fix, Trix!
Lesson 4: Time to Share, Claire!

Anchor Book: An anchor book is used to introduce the topic. The teacher reads the book aloud and the class discusses how effectively the book promotes or invites the strategy.

Planning Sheet: There is a planning sheet provided for each lesson. The teacher explains the sheet and the students are given time to work independently on it. Encourage students to complete filling out the sheet prior to the next lesson. Teachers may choose to adapt these sheets to better meet the needs of their particular grades or classes.

Lesson 2: Writing (Guided and Independent)

See page 42 for a list of technique lessons.

You will find many examples of teacher models throughout this book.

Share: Each lesson begins with students in partners sharing their planning sheet.

Writing Technique: Each lesson will focus on a specific writing technique. A technique is introduced once, but will recur in subsequent lessons.

Teacher Model: The teacher models how to take ideas from the planning sheet and begin to develop them into a piece of writing using the writing technique.

Student Write: Students begin writing their drafts. Depending on the grade level, this could be from 10 to 20 minutes of quiet writing.

Teacher Circulates: During writing time, the teacher can either circulate through the room or conduct individual conferences with students.

Lesson 3: Conferencing and Editing

See page 23 for a reproducible version of the Writing Power Conference Record.

Conferences (A Star, A Wish, and a Think): Each week students conference with a partner, reading aloud their latest piece of writing. The focus of this conference is not only to give compliments and suggestions, but also to practice their thinking. While students are working with partners, the teacher can hold individual conferences with one or two students each week.

Editing: Students work independently to edit their writing using an editing checklist (see page 20).

Lesson 4: Publishing and Sharing

We all know how busy the week gets, especially when weeks are cut short due to holidays or professional development days. While it is important for students to go through the first three stages with their weekly writing, Day 4 is not always necessary. In the lessons presented in the third section of this book, Days 3 and 4 are general, and are not detailed for each lesson.

Publishing: Producing a "good copy" or a published piece is optional and will depend on the grade level. It is not necessary for every piece to be published. While we encourage children to publish some of their writing, the good copy becomes less important, moving us toward a focus on process rather than product.

Sharing: Three or four students are selected each week to share their writing piece with the class. Students can volunteer for sharing, or a rotation system can be established.

The Lesson Framework in Action

Organizing

Donald Graves and Lucy Calkins first introduced us to the writer's notebook—a special notebook, separate from other language arts activities, that is used for supporting the belief that writers need to constantly be ready, pencil in hand, to record thoughts, moments, snippets of life that may later be used in pieces of writing. *Notebook Know-How* by Aimee Buckner was a welcome reminder of important aspects of a writer's work: developing ideas, brainstorming, organizing thoughts. For a few years, I splurged and bought my students small bound notebooks because I wanted them to feel that a writer's notebook is special, different from other school exercise books. But while I loved the idea of the writer's notebook being an actual notebook, the novelty of having a real writer's notebook wore thin when I had to lug 27 of them home with me to mark. I also found that many students were not used to the confinement of smaller pages; the size of the notebook made the actual process of writing feel awkward for many and made marking next to impossible for me.

Unsuccessful experiences led me to a rather boring but more practical solution for keeping track of plans, drafts, and extra sheets: the dependable duotang. I recognize that we all develop our own ways of having students keep track of their writing and that some may still feel the real notebook is a way of promoting real writers. But duotangs (or thin three-ring binders) make it easier for students to add and remove pages, and also to organize their writing into sections for each strategy.

Conferencing

Reading aloud your writing to someone else is an excellent way to hear what your writing sounds like. Donald Graves introduced conferencing as one of the steps in the writing process. Teacher conferences are opportunities for students to spend one-on-one time with their teachers to talk about their writing. The teacher can use this time to do some informal assessment or to encourage or nudge students to work on a particular aspect of their writing.

Partner conferences are another way for students to share their writing. In my experience, these paired conferences are often not as effective as they could be unless the teacher takes the time to train students and give them specific guidelines. It is my preference to have conferencing time immediately before editing, as often students will spot mistakes while they are reading aloud that they may have missed when reading silently.

I have always liked the "two stars and a wish" approach that gives students a specific way to respond after their partner has shared their writing. Since Writing Power is focusing on the reader's thinking, I have adapted this response to include a "think":

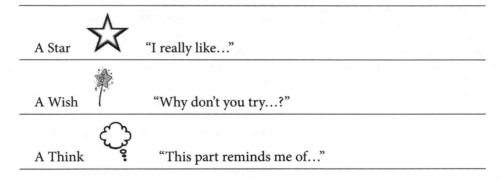

A Star	"I really like…"
A Wish	"Why don't you try…?"
A Think	"This part reminds me of…"

The first time you introduce conferencing to your students, it is important that you model what each of the responses looks and sounds like by giving examples of each. See page 19 for the Writing Conference Guideline chart. When working with a partner in a conference situation, students need to be given guidelines for each role in the conference: the reader and the listener. Again, it is important for a teacher to be explicit about the do's and don't's of conferencing and what a conference looks like.

WRITING CONFERENCE GUIDELINES

The Reader

DO's	**DON'T's**
✓ Have your paper flat on the table **between** you and your partner when you are reading.	x Don't hold your paper up in front of your face when you are reading.
✓ Read in a loud, clear voice.	x Don't mumble.
✓ If you find a mistake when reading, mark it quickly with a pencil so you can find it later and then continue reading.	x Don't stop and do a lot of editing while you are reading .

The Listener

DO's	**DON'T's**
✓ Look at the page and follow while your partner is reading.	x Don't look at or work on your own paper while your partner is reading.
✓ Give your partner your respect and full attention while he/she is reading.	x Don't look around, talk, or play while your partner is reading.
✓ After your partner has finished reading, give a "star" (compliment), a "wish" (suggestions) and a "think" (share your thinking).	x Don't stay silent when your partner is finished reading.
	x Don't criticize or say something unkind.

Editing

I can still remember getting writing back from teachers in elementary and high school covered in red pen marks. Comments such as "not clear," "watch your spelling," and "needs work" did little to boost my confidence or move me forward in my writing. Editing is a step in the writing process, and therefore should be taught and practiced in classrooms. In my experience with trying to teach students how to revise their own writing, however, there is one small problem: kids hate editing. Despite our efforts to teach them how, giving them checklist after checklist, they might change the odd word or add a period here or there—but let's not kid ourselves. When it comes right down to it, when it comes to editing, most kids fake it!

Modeling has become an important aspect of teaching writing and so it should be considered an important component of teaching students how to edit. Telling students that their writing "needs work" does not provide enough explicit information to help them make the appropriate changes to improve their writing. At the same time, providing them with an editing checklist of, say, seventeen things to check for is not going to prove effective either. Editing needs to be broken down into clear, specific steps so that students know exactly how and what to fix. Modeling these steps for students on your own piece of writing will help make the process more manageable. Before beginning the process of editing, it's important that students understand why editing is an important stage in the writing process.

From my perspective, there are two aspects to a piece of writing: what it *looks like* and what it *sounds like*. Both are important areas of editing that need to be addressed, but we need to separate them when going through the editing process. What a piece of writing looks like deals with the conventions: spelling, grammar, punctuation, and neatness. One might refer to this as writing etiquette, or politeness to the reader. Students need to understand the importance of going back to proofread and making appropriate changes so that their writing can be read. This might be considered the proofreading component of editing.

What a piece of writing sounds like is the other consideration during the editing process. This aspect of editing is a little more complex, but the crucial question is this: Does it sound as good as it could? Here we are faced with the challenge of having to reorganize and rearrange sentences to make them sound better, flow better, or make better sense. More effort is involved, as it is more of a challenge to rearrange a sentence than it is to change a "d" to a "D" or to add a period. Children are reluctant self-editors. They pretty much consider the writing complete with the first draft and, while they tolerate having to go through their writing to add capitals and periods, they are rarely chomping at the bit to reorganize and rework their sentences.

I still cringe at the memory of teachers who made me write a rough copy, second draft, third draft, and good copy. By the time I was writing a piece for a fourth time, I had lost all interest in it. Too much of a good thing—or anything—can drain our enthusiasm. But spending time reworking a piece of writing is an important part of the writing process and students need to be taught specific ways to do this effectively. Setting specific guidelines or checklists for editing can help make the process less obscure:

- Make the checklist manageable and keep the number of steps to a minimum.
- Have students number their edits (using a small number in a circle beside the correction) so you can quickly check to see if they are following the guidelines and doing more than just correcting spelling and punctuation.
- Model! Model! Model! If we want our students to revise their writing then we need to show them how to do it.

Here are my examples of editing checklists for primary and intermediate levels. While you can adapt them to fit the needs of your class, they show how much less intimidating and more manageable a short editing checklist can be.

This editing checklist is for intermediate students. An example of a *word change* is finding a word such as "hot" and changing it to "sweltering." Teachers should model several examples of this. See page 48 for the lesson on "triple-scoop" words.

3, 2, 1…Edit!

- **3** spelling and/or **3** punctuation corrections

- **2** word changes

- **1** sentence rearranged

This editing checklist is for primary students.

1, 2, 3, 4—Edit!

1. **Fix** spelling and punctuation.

2. **Change** a word that doesn't sound right.

3. **Erase** a word (or words) that doesn't fit.

4. **Add** a word (or words) to make your writing better.

Assessment

"The only way to raise the quality of writing in school is to create, share, and celebrate the specific criteria for that quality with everybody on a regular basis."
—Barry Lane

See pages 24–27 for Writing Power Assessment Rubrics for Grades 1 through 7.

For the rubrics on pages 24–27, I use the benchmarks NY (Not Yet meeting expectations), M (Meeting expectations), FM (Fully Meeting expectations), and EX (EXceeding expectations). Feel free to substitute your own terms for learning benchmarks.

Students who are developing writing skills have an enormous amount to think about. Early primary students who are just beginning to form legible letters are not at a place in their development where composing and constructing lengthy writing pieces is a primary concern. It may be just enough for them to write the initial consonant of a word. However, the Grade 1 students at my school proved to me that even they are capable of learning writing techniques and can understand the difference, say, between a "climbing" story and a "walking" story (see Chapter 4: Narrative Power). More proficient writers are now expected not only to spell all words correctly, indent, and have neat printing, but also to apply the many aspects of good writing, such as voice and organization, to their assignments.

Writing is concrete, and therefore easier to assess than more abstract actions like, for example, the thinking aspect of reading. Writing assessment, as discussed earlier in this book, has come a long way from the red-pen–marking days of my education, when spelling, grammar, and mechanics were the only things that were really considered or measured. Thankfully, using such important tools as performance standards and the six traits of writing, teachers have moved forward to the point where they know that writing assessment requires a more evenly distributed assessment of both skills and mechanics, meaning and style. With many schools conducting school-wide writing assessments in the fall and spring, teachers are becoming more familiar with the idea that assessment drives our practice—where I see there are gaps in my students' learning, I am responsible for filling those gaps with effective instruction. No longer is assessment solely for the purpose of recording marks in thin green marks books; now it is used to inform us of what to teach next. When teachers can assess their students' writing and notice that most of them are struggling with an aspect of writing, then they know that the next few mini-lessons should focus on that aspect.

Many school districts have implemented or are moving toward implementing school-wide writes, administrated in the fall and spring of each school year. Fall results help to formulate benchmarks and guide teachers to plan writing lessons to support their students' needs. Spring assessments help teachers to see the growth and development in their students' writing. Teachers commonly meet in grade groups and use established provincial performance standards as their guide for evaluating these writing samples.

Ongoing assessment of weekly classroom writing is also important in guiding our practice and moving our students forward. The rubrics that start on page 24 are not intended to replace any performance standards that your school district has set. My intent is that they be used to evaluate the weekly writing your students are doing. Regular checks on where your students are can help guide your practice and also provide ongoing feedback to your students so they know where they are and which specific areas may require more attention. Setting regular goals for improving writing skills can help both students and teachers move forward.

Writing Power Weekly Planning

Date: _____

Strategy: _____   TERM   1   2   3

Weekly Writing Focus: _____

Lesson 1: Plan	Lesson 2: Write	Lesson 3: Conference/ Edit	Lesson 4: Share/ Publish
Anchor Book(s):	New Writing Technique:	Editing Focus: • • •	Students Sharing: • • • Publishing: YES NO
Planning Page:	Other Techniques:		
Notes:	Notes:	Teacher conference with • • •	Notes:

Writing Power Conference Record

Student: _____ DATE: _____ TERM: 1 2 3

Writing Focus: _____

Teacher	Record student response
What is the thinking strategy that we have been focusing on in our writing (and reading)?	
What writing technique have we been working on? Can you tell me a little bit about this technique?	
Do you remember your writing goal from our last conference? What have you been working on?	
Go ahead and read your piece out loud.	Teacher Notes:
Can you tell me what part of this piece you are most proud of and why?	
Can you tell me one part of this piece that you think might need some work and why?	
I'm noticing that you have really done a good job of…	Possible suggestions: *Circle one or two* • Beginning/ ending • Using writing techniques • Organization: ideas are grouped together • Adding details (not "robot writing") • Using "triple-scoop words" • Including the senses • Using capitals and periods • Variety of sentences • Voice • Other: _____
Here's something I think might help your writing to get even better…	Possible suggestions: *Circle one or two* • Beginning/ ending • Using writing techniques • Organization: ideas are grouped together • Adding details (not "robot writing") • Using "triple-scoop words" • Including the senses • Using capitals and periods • Variety of sentences • Voice • Other: _____
Let's set a new goal for your writing. What do you think would help your writing get even better?	Record student's goal here:

Pembroke Publishers ©2011 *Writing Power* by Adrienne Gear ISBN 978-1-55138-263-0

Writing Power Assessment Rubrics

Name: _____   Date: _____

Grade 1 Writing Assessment	NY	M	FM	EX
• Is able to generate ideas for writing independently				
• Is attempting to support an idea with a detail				
• Is attempting new writing techniques, such as voice and simile				
• Stays on topic and groups similar ideas together				
• Uses growing awareness of sounds (beginning, middle, and end) to write words				
• Uses appropriate spacing between words and forms letters legibly				

Writing Goal: _____

Name: _____   Date: _____

Grade 2 Writing Assessment	NY	M	FM	EX
• Is able to generate writing that makes sense and is easy to follow				
• Can support an idea with details and examples				
• Is attempting to use writing techniques, such as voice, anchor lines, and similes				
• Stays on topic and groups ideas together				
• Is beginning to use capitals and periods correctly				
• Uses phonetic spelling to write independently				
• Is beginning to edit punctuation and spelling with guidance				
• Is developing writing that engages the reader to *_____				

* Choose applicable strategy: *make connections, visualize, ask questions, make inferences, transform their thinking*

Writing Goal: _____

Pembroke Publishers ©2011 *Writing Power* by Adrienne Gear ISBN 978-1-55138-263-0

Name: _____   Date: _____

Grade 3 Writing Assessment	NY	M	FM	EX
• Is able to generate writing that flows smoothly and makes sense				
• Can support an idea with details, examples, and feelings				
• Is including writing techniques, such as voice, anchor lines, and similes				
• Stays on topic and groups ideas together using complete sentences				
• Is attempting to include more interesting sentences and language				
• Spells most high-frequency words correctly and is moving toward conventional spelling				
• Is developing an awareness that knowing how good readers think can enhance their writing				
• Is developing writing that engages the reader to *_____				

* Choose applicable strategy: *make connections, visualize, ask questions, make inferences, transform their thinking*

Writing goal: _____

Name: _____   Date: _____

Grade 4 Writing Assessment	NY	M	FM	EX
• Is learning to generate writing that flows smoothly, makes sense, and engages the reader				
• Organizes and groups ideas in logical sequence and paragraphs				
• Can support an idea with details, examples, and feelings				
• Is including writing techniques, such as voice, anchor lines, and similes				
• Is attempting to include more interesting sentences and language				
• Writes complete, legible sentences with few errors				
• Is beginning to edit for spelling, punctuation, and minor sentence revision				
• Is developing an awareness that knowing how good readers think can enhance their writing				
• Is developing writing that engages the reader to *_____				

* Choose applicable strategy: *make connections, visualize, ask questions, make inferences, transform their thinking*

Writing Goal: _____

Pembroke Publishers ©2011 *Writing Power* by Adrienne Gear ISBN 978-1-55138-263-0

Name: _____   Date: _____

Grade 5 Writing Assessment	NY	M	FM	EX
• Is able to generate writing that flows smoothly, makes sense, and engages the reader				
• Is using paragraphs to organize ideas				
• Supports ideas with details, examples, and feelings				
• Is incorporating a variety of writing techniques independently				
• Uses strong verbs and interesting language; is experimenting with dialogue				
• Writes complete, legible sentences with few errors				
• Edits for punctuation, spelling, and grammar; revises to enhance ideas				
• Is developing an awareness that knowing how good readers think can enhance their writing				
• Is developing writing that engages the reader to* _____				

* Choose applicable strategy: *make connections, visualize, ask questions, make inferences, transform their thinking*

Writing Goal: _____

Name: _____   Date: _____

Grade 6 Writing Assessment	NY	M	FM	EX
• Is able to generate writing that flows smoothly, makes sense, and engages the reader				
• Develops stories with plots that include characters, problems, and solutions				
• Can support an idea with details, examples, and feelings				
• Uses a variety of writing techniques, including similes, personification, anchor lines, and sensory imagery				
• Is experimenting with sentence lengths and more complex sentence structure				
• Writes complete, legible sentences with few errors				
• Edits for punctuation, spelling, and grammar with greater precision				
• Is developing writing that engages the reader to make * _____				

* Choose applicable strategy: *make connections, visualize, ask questions, make inferences, transform their thinking*

Writing Goal: _____

Pembroke Publishers ©2011 *Writing Power* by Adrienne Gear ISBN 978-1-55138-263-0

Name: _____   Date: _____

Grade 7 Writing Assessment	NY	M	FM	EX
• Is able to generate writing that is well-organized, flows smoothly, and makes sense				
• Develops stories that show character development, dialogue, and a clearly established beginning, problem, and solution				
• Is able to support an idea with details, examples, and feelings				
• Uses a variety of writing techniques effectively, including similes, personification, and sensory imagery				
• Is experimenting with sentence lengths and more complex sentence structure				
• Constructs sentences that are complete, are legible, and have few errors				
• Independently edits for punctuation, spelling, and grammar with greater precision				
• Shows a greater awareness of audience and is developing writing that engages the reader to make * _____				

* Choose applicable strategy: *make connections, visualize, ask questions, make inferences, transform their thinking*

Writing Goal: _____

Pembroke Publishers ©2011 *Writing Power* by Adrienne Gear ISBN 978-1-55138-263-0

The Big Picture

When I first started teaching, I loved visiting teacher resource stores that provided me with an endless supply of lessons to fill my day. "Canned" or pre-prepared writing lessons were among my favorites: a "story starter" or mystery topic that grabbed the students' attention and got them excited about writing. Then off they would go to write, leaving me with perhaps 15 minutes to catch my breath. And while the students appeared to be excited about the topic and did produce adequate pieces of writing, I realize that what those random, isolated writing lessons collected in a writing folder lacked was a sense of the bigger picture: Why am I writing? How can I use my own ideas to stimulate the ideas of others? How can I use my own experiences as a source for writing ideas? What writing techniques can I use to better engage my reader?

After almost 20 years in the profession, I am constantly asking myself: What is the purpose of this lesson? How does this lesson fit into a bigger picture? Before I teach my students anything, I want them to know why they are learning it and how it fits into a more expansive idea of learning; teaching writing is no exception. I no longer assign isolated writing lessons to my students, but instead try to ensure that every writing lesson I teach is a piece of the bigger picture. So it is important that, before launching into the specific strategy lessons, teachers spend time teaching some big-picture lessons: the purpose for writing; sources for writing; types of writing; and tools for writing. These concept lessons help your students see what being a writer is, so that the writing lessons that follow make more sense because they fit into this greater whole.

3 The Power to Invite Readers to Think

A New Term: Alocognition

Metacognition, or awareness of thinking, is the underlying foundation of comprehension instruction. Teaching students to be aware of their thinking and to develop a language to articulate thinking is the foundation of Reading Power. How then can we use this awareness of thinking to help us become better writers? Developing an awareness, as a writer, of your readers' cognitive response to and engagement with your writing is the underlying foundation of Writing Power. By helping writers become aware of their readers' thinking, we will be adding a new perspective, purpose, and depth to writing. We can enhance not only our students' ability to write, but also their understanding about the relationship between reader and writer.

In developing this idea, my problem was finding a word that meant "awareness of my readers' thinking" (as opposed to "awareness of my own thinking"). The word *metacognition* means "self thinking": *meta* comes from the Greek root for "self" and *cognition* is understanding and thinking. There does not appear, however, to be a word that means "being aware of others' thinking." I consulted, without success, friends and colleagues (thank you Cheryl, Kimberly, Sue, Andrew, Michelle, Duncan, Donna, Rob, Edward, Janet, Cay, and Cay's grad student). I searched in vain through hundreds of websites on words and definitions. So for the purpose of writing this book, I have taken the liberty of coining my own phrase.

It is important that there is no confusion between *alocognition* and *telepathy*. Telepathy refers to the ability to determine what someone else is thinking. Alocognition is having an awareness that someone else is thinking.

Since *alos* is the Greek root for "other" and *cognition* means understanding and thinking, *alos-cognition* seemed to fit. After a lot of thought and saying the word out loud for several hours, I dropped the "s" and have now settled on *alocognition*. And so I introduce you to the word *alocognition,* which means "having an awareness of the thinking of others."

Teachers who have already integrated a metacognitive approach into their reading instruction have, in fact, laid the groundwork for Writing Power: teaching writing that will more effectively engage a reader's thinking. The language and the strategies in Writing Power are the same as for Reading Power, except this time we're looking at it through a different lens—through the writer's lens rather than the reader's. So the profile of a proficient reader that we have become familiar with can be flipped over to reveal the other side of the coin.

Foundation of Reading Power	Foundation of Writing Power
Metacognition: an awareness of my own thinking	**Alocognition:** an awareness of others' thinking
Good readers are aware of their own thinking when they read. They know that in order to find meaning in what they are reading, they can make connections, visualize, ask questions, make inferences, and transform their thinking.	Good writers are aware that readers think while they read. As good writers, we want to ensure that our writing engages our readers and invites them to make connections, visualize, ask questions, make inferences, and transform their thinking.

Lesson: What Writers Need to Know

Just as I encourage all teachers who use Reading Power in their classrooms to begin with an introductory lesson that introduces students to the overall concept of readers as thinkers and metacognition, I encourage the same to introduce the concept of Writing Power. I want students to understand the concept of alocognition, becoming more aware of *why* they write and that their readers are going to be *thinking* about their writing.

- Begin the lesson:

  This year, we are going to be doing a lot of writing in our class. Today I want to spend a little bit of time talking about writers.

- Ask students, "Why do writer's write?" (You might get a wide range of answers here!) Explain to students that some people write diaries and journals, which is a private kind of writing. But, most often, writers write because they have ideas they want to share with other people.

  Writing is a way of giving a small piece of yourself to somebody else—and that somebody else is anybody who is going to read your writing. To me, a book is a gift from the writer. When I open up a book, it feels like I'm opening up a present—and I never know what the present might be. Sometimes the book is so good I feel as though it is the greatest present and I want to say thank you to the writer for "gifting me" with their words and their ideas.

  Now I want to talk about readers for a minute. Readers are very important to writers. Writers need readers. Why? (because without readers, there would be nobody to read your writing) What do good readers do when they read?

  (For those students familiar with Reading Power, this conversation can review the Reading Power strategies.)

  When I read something funny I might laugh; I might cry or feel sad if I read something sad; I might feel suspense. When I read something, I might start making a connection, or visualizing, asking a question, or making an inference. I might even start to think about something in a different way. When I read, I *think*! Writing is very powerful because it invites readers to think. Good writers want their readers

BOOK by George Ella Lyon invites readers into the pages, asking the question: "Readers, look at the book you have just opened…what is it you hold in your hands?" It is no longer in print; however, if you can find it in your library, it can be a wonderful addition to this lesson.

The phrase "gifted me" originated from Carrie Gleason, extraordinary primary teacher at Admiral Seymour Elementary School. When one of her students writes something extraordinary or surprising, she will say, "_____ (student's name) gifted me with his/her writing today."

to think; they want to write in such a way that their readers think, feel, laugh, cry, make connections, ask questions, visualize, infer, and transform their thinking. From now on, when we write, we are not only going to be thinking about *how* to write or *what* we write, but also *why* we write. We are going to be thinking about our readers and trying to make sure our writing invites them to think.

Invitation

If you are a dreamer, come in.
If you are a dreamer, a wisher, a liar,
A hope-er, a pray-er, a magic bean buyer…
If you're a pretender, come sit by my fire,
For we have some flax golden tales to spin.
Come in!
Come in!
—Shel Silverstein

- Read the poem "Invitation" by Shel Silverstein.
- With students, discuss who the invitation is from and who it is to. Discuss what "Come in! Come in!" means.
- Show a party invitation. Ask the students what it is, when they might get one.
- Explain that, like Shel Silverstein, you are going to be inviting your readers to think by making "thinking invitations" for them. Explain that a thinking invitation is an invitation to readers to think when they read your writing. Students can fold a blank sheet of paper twice to make an invitation. Students can either copy the information from the board or make up their own.

> *Cover*: Come to a Thinking Party!
> *Inside*
> You are invited to a Thinking Party.
> Where: Inside your head.
> When: Whenever you read my writing
> Please Bring: Your thinking! (connections, questions, visual images, inferences, transformed thoughts)
> Hope you can come!
> RSVP to _____ (student's name)

4 Thinking Power: Sources for Writing Ideas

Finding ideas for writing can be a challenge. While many suggestions for helping students find ideas for writing have come and gone over the years, getting started on a piece of writing and staring at a blank piece of paper or a blank screen still proves to be a challenge for the best of us. Using writing workshop, we encouraged young writers to write from their own experiences, to observe the world around them through "a writer's lens," and to record special moments and memories in their writer's notebooks to be later expanded into larger pieces. Journal writing became a popular way of encouraging students to write about personal experiences; however, often these were nothing but "bed-to-bed" stories (*I got up, I did this, I did that, I did this, and then I went to bed*), recorded lists of daily activities that became a chore and a bore to read. While we might use the common term "writing from experiences" with our students, what exactly does this mean to a seven-year-old? Brain Pockets provide a visual concept for students to see how our experiences are a source for generating ideas in our writing.

Brain Pockets

The idea of Brain Pockets first evolved from my work in reading comprehension. I had a student in my class who was rather unusual. He demonstrated a different way of being in the world and, while I found myself wanting to embrace his differences, for the most part I found them to be quite distracting during my lessons. When he raised his hand, I avoided eye contact. I knew from past experience that what would emerge from his mouth would result in an outburst of laughter from the class, along with some eye-rolling. By the time everyone was settled down, the focus of the lesson would be lost.

One particular discussion was centred around a lesson on inferring. The students were observing a photograph from the newspaper and using the clues to infer what might be going on. This student put up his hand and I reluctantly called upon him to share his inference: "I think that maybe the aliens are about to land across the bay because they want to suck up all the grandmothers from earth and take them to Planet Phu-phu." You can imagine how the rest of the class received his response.

On a sudden whim, I went to the board and drew a large brain. I divided the brain into three equal parts. I said, in a slightly exasperated voice,

Our brains are powerful because they control our bodies and hold our thoughts. A brain has three major compartments that store thoughts. They are called Brain Pockets. First is our Memory Pocket. It holds memories and experiences and the feelings connected to those experiences. Second is our Fact Pocket; it holds facts and information. Third is our Imagination Pocket. It is a place filled with imaginary and creative thoughts. Our Brain Pockets help us when we are reading and thinking. We use the memories, the facts, and the imagination to help us understand what we are reading. Depending on what we are reading or thinking about, we visit different pockets. For example, if I am reading a book about friendship, I might go to my Memory Pocket because I might have had a similar experience with my own friend. If we are reading a book about volcanoes, I might go into my Fact Pocket to find some information I already know about volcanoes.

I then explained to the student that I noticed he spent much of his time in his Imagination Pocket, but that sometimes he needed to visit the other pockets. A few days later, this student approached my desk during quiet reading. "Ms. Gear, I've been thinking about what you told us about our Brain Pockets. And you know you my Imagination Pocket?"

"Yes," I replied.

"Well…I think I live there."

Acknowledging and giving language to different ways of thinking has helped many students identify the sources for their thinking. And while it doesn't prevent all from entering the wrong pocket, it has helped students recognize the difference. And I have found myself becoming far less bothered by a student who strays into the wrong pocket because I am now able to guide him or her to a different place in their thinking.

Developing this awareness of our brains as sources for developing and deepening our understanding has become an essential part of supporting and guiding my students to add their own thoughts to what they are reading. In terms of writing, I realized that Brain Pockets can also become an important way of discussing the notion that writers find ideas for writing by tapping into their own stored experiences.

Lesson: Introducing Brain Pockets

- Begin the lesson:

  One of the important things about being a writer is finding ideas for things to write about that will be interesting for our readers. Today we're going to talk about where writers get their ideas for writing.

- Ask students where writers get their ideas (from things they know, experiences, imagination).

  These ideas are stored in a writer's brain. Our brains may be small but they are incredible places because not only do they control our bodies, but they are like a huge storage place for our thoughts. Our brains have three pockets to store thoughts: a Memory Pocket, a Fact Pocket, and an Imagination Pocket.

  (Draw a quick visual of a brain with three sections)

  When we read, we use these pockets to help us understand what we are reading. When we write, we use these pockets to help us find ideas to write about. Today, we're going to create personalized Brain Pockets. We're going to fill each pocket with personal memories, facts, and things from our imagination.

The Grade 6 teachers at Crofton House elementary school in Vancouver used the idea of Brain Pockets with their students for their visual journals. They created their own personal visual for their Brain Pockets, filling each pocket with their own individual experiences, knowledge, and imagination.

- Model the Brain Pocket example on chart paper or the board. Use a blank image of a brain and record ideas in each of the pockets.

Teacher Model

Memory Pocket (people, places, events, pets)	Fact Pocket (things I know a lot about)	Imagination Pocket (things I imagine)
• Spencer and Oliver • My sisters, mum, dad • Sumo, my cat • Christmas, Halloween • Summer holidays on Mayne Island • Hiking in Manning Park • My first bad haircut	• Reading • Children's books • Hockey • Flowers • Baking • Poetry • Weather • Winter Olympics	• Sleeping on a cloud • Being able to fly • Being invisible • Being able to talk to animals • A talking highlighter pen

- Create and copy a Brain Pocket organizer to pass out to students. Students can draw or write to fill each pocket.

This sample is by a Grade 3 student.

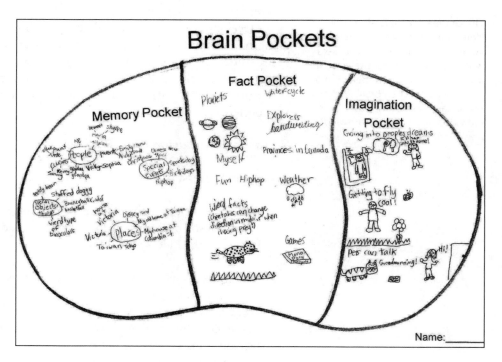

- End the lesson:

Brain pockets help us when we're reading and when we're writing. When we're reading, we can find things inside our brain to help us understand the text better. When we write, we can use the ideas from our brain pockets to help us find things to write about. We add new things to our brain pockets every day.

5 Narrative Power: Types of Writing

Just as the first *Reading Power* book focused on helping students read and understand fiction texts, I wanted this first *Writing Power* book to focus on writing fiction. You would be right to guess that this book might well be followed by a Nonfiction Writing Power book!

While information, or nonfiction, writing is an important aspect of writing instruction in schools, this book focuses on teaching the writing of fiction: writing from personal experiences, writing stories, and writing poems.

We are all familiar with the various forms of fiction, including personal narrative, stories, and poems; however, the writing guidelines for these genres have always been a bit muddy for me. Up until a few years ago, I was under the impression that there was only one text structure for fiction writing—the story. Children, from a very early age, are introduced to the specific elements or components of a fictional text structure, which include characters, setting; beginning, middle, end; problem, solution. Fairy tales are classic examples of this text structure and are often used to help students learn to identify the specific elements of a story. And while this text structure becomes relatively familiar territory for students to identify when reading, it is a greater challenge to master when it comes to writing. Effectively incorporating all the specific elements of a story is a challenge for even the most gifted of writers, and I am sometimes puzzled as to why we spend so much time trying to teach children how to write a story.

Text Structures

I will be forever grateful to Susan Van Blarcom, well-respected teacher at Crofton House Elementary School; she suggested to me that fiction texts consist of two text structures, rather than one. After sifting this thought through the hectic and busy place I call my brain for more than a year, I realized she was absolutely correct. There are, indeed, two distinct structures of fictional writing: one, the familiar story structure as described above; the other, a more linear structure. A linear structure is that form of writing that does not focus on specific characters, setting, or a specific problem and solution, but that instead develops in a linear structure around a topic, and includes descriptions and often a repeating line or phrase. In a linear piece of text, one could say that thoughts and ideas are shared, but nothing really happens. Nonfiction text structures can also be classified under this linear structure if one is writing, for example, a descriptive report about an animal or country, or instructions on how to plant a seed.

Now, although we can agree that both these structures can be applied to virtually all writing that students are instructed in, they are indeed very different writing forms and I believe they need to be introduced to students as such. So, to simplify things for myself and my students (something that I am always trying to do), I have categorized the two main story text structures as Walking Stories and Climbing Stories.

- Walking Stories move along a straight line, are often on a theme or topic, and include descriptions and examples. This is a common structure for nonfiction, as well as many picture books.
- Climbing Stories, on the other hand, begin with a character and a setting, and move along for a short period of time—but then, something happens. When the problem is introduced, the story starts to climb uphill. Once you reach the top of the hill, you need to find a way down, so the writer solves the problem and the story comes back down to where it started. This climb up and down is a simplified way of explaining a plot line.

The other text structure introduced in this book is poetry. Poetry follows, of course, a very different set of criteria, including shorter lines, rhythm, rhyme, repetition. Many of the writing techniques introduced in this book for use in fictional writing are also important techniques for writing poetry.

Introducing these text structures to students early in the year will bring clarity and understanding as they learn to develop their ability to write fiction.

See pages 37–39 for the lessons to introduce these text structures.

TEXT STRUCTURES

Walking Stories Start _ _ _ / _ _ _ / _ _ _ / _ _ _ / _ _ _ End	Climbing Stories Start _ _ _ but then _ _ _ End	Poems
• Based on a topic or theme • Include details, descriptions, and examples • Nothing specific "happens" • Often have no main character, beginning, middle, end, problem, or solution • Often include a repeating phrase or anchor line throughout	• Based on a character and what happens to that character • Usually have a specific setting • Have a clear beginning, middle, and end • Include a specific problem and solution • Follow a plot line	• Based on a topic or theme • Include details, descriptions, and examples • Have short lines • Sometimes rhyme • Can have repetition • Say something old in a brand new way

P = primary
I = intermediate

The Poppleton series for beginning readers by Cynthia Rylant are excellent models of climbing stories for early primary students.

Here are some examples of the text structures at work. Many of the examples of walking stories are picture books; I often use them with intermediate students when my purpose is to model or introduce a writing technique.

Books Showing Kinds of Narrative Power

WALKING STORIES

Anthony Browne, *My Dad* (P)
Jamie Lee Curtis, *When I Was Little* (P)
Jenny Offill, *17 Things I'm Not Allowed to Do Anymore* (P)
Amy Krouse Rosenthal, *The OK Book* (P)

Cynthia Rylant, *Snow* (I)
Cynthia Rylant, *When I Was Young in the Mountains* (I)
David Shannon, *No, David* (P, I)
Judith Viorst, *Alexander and the Terrible, Horrible, No Good, Very Bad Day* (P, I)

36   *The Big Picture*

CLIMBING STORIES

Little Red Riding Hood (any version) (P, I)
Eve Bunting, *Fly Away Home* (P, I)
Sherry Garland, *The Lotus Seed* (I)
Kevin Henkes, *Lily and the Purple Plastic Purse* (P, I)
Ann McGovern, *The Lady in the Box* (I)
Robert Munsch, *The Paper Bag Princess* (P, I)
Chris Raschka, *Yo! Yes!* (I)
Cynthia Rylant, *Poppleton* (chapter 1: Neighbors) (P)

POETRY ANTHOLOGIES

Elise Paschen (ed), *Poetry Speaks to Children* (book and CD)
Jack Prelutsky and Arnold Lobel (eds), *Random House Book of Poetry*
Jack Prelutsky and Meilo So (eds), *The 20th Century Children's Poetry Treasury*
Mary Michaels White, et al (eds), *Sing a Song of Popcorn*

Story Strips

An approach similar to Story Strips is Book Making, developed by educational consultant and author Matt Glover. Stephanie Yorath, Grade 1 teacher at Croften House School in Vancouver, uses this approach in her writing workshop. Her students are given a blank book to write their story in, rather than a blank page to write on. Each new story is written in a new book, instilling the notion of real writers writing real books for real readers.

Walking Story Strips can also be used for nonfiction writing. Wendy Hugali's Grade 1 students at Sexsmith Elementary wrote about their field trip to the aquarium using the story strips. Each box was used to describe a different thing the children did, saw, learned, and liked.

Story strips can also be used with older students to help them plan and organize their ideas. Each box or section of the story strip represents a new paragraph in the story and can be expanded by adding details and examples.

Beginning writers need support in keeping their ideas organized and learning the two narrative structures. Providing primary writers with blank story strips has proven successful for helping students develop their sense of story and distinguish between the walking and climbing writing forms.

The Climbing Story Strip (see page 41) is used to teach emergent writers the elements of a story (characters, setting, problem, solution) and to introduce the idea of a plot line. The Walking Story Strips (page 40) are used when students are writing a descriptive piece: each frame contains a different aspect of the description or piece of information, but nothing really happens in terms of a significant problem.

On page 40, the first Walking Story Strip has spaces for four pictures, while the second Walking Story Strip has space for only one large image. Depending on the topic, teachers can use one or the other. A piece about fall might have a description of four aspects of the season—the weather, special celebrations, things I like to do, sounds and smells of fall—which correspond with four different pictures. A piece, for example, about My Dragon might require only one large picture.

Lesson: Introducing Walking and Climbing Stories

• Begin the lesson:

Even though every story we read is different, stories usually follow the same pathway. We call the path of a story the story structure. Some stories stay on a flat path.

(Draw a horizontal line on the board)

We call these "walking stories." Walking stories are usually stories that describe a person, a place, or a thing. The writer includes lots of details about the topic and there is often anchor line, or repeating phrase, holding the writing steady.

The other kind of story is called a "climbing story." These are the stories that start out on a straight path for a while—but then, all of a sudden something happens!

(Draw a flat line and then angle the line up like the side of a mountain)

The straight part of the path at the beginning is usually where the writer introduces us to a character, then the story starts to climb up when something happens. You might notice a story beginning to climb up when a writer says "One day…" or "Suddenly…" Now, a writer knows that they can't just leave a reader stranded up here at the top of the mountain, not knowing what happens. So the writer has to explain how the problem gets solved, to bring the reader back down the path again. Once the path reaches the bottom, the story is over. When you write a climbing story, you need to follow this pathway: step-step-up-up-down.

- Model a walking story.

Teacher Model

Walking Story: *Snow*
Snow is sparkly and cold. Snow falls silently and covers my yard with a white blanket. Snow gives birds a chance to make footprints. Snow is the magic of winter.

Explain that this is a walking story because the writer talks about one thing (snow) and gives a lot of details and descriptions about the snow; however, nothing really happens, so we stay on a straight line.

- Model a climbing story:

Teacher Model

Climbing Story: *George Gets Lost*
George the monkey lived in the jungle with his mother and his brother. George loved to swing from the trees with his tail and pick ticks from his little brothers fur.

Explain that this is the flat part of the story: the character is introduced with some examples and details.

One day, George got lost in the jungle.
Now, something happens and the story is starting to climb up.
He looked everywhere for his mother and his brother but he could not find them. George climbed a tree and started to cry.
We can't stop the story here or our reader will get mad and say, "But then what happened to George?" So we need to solve the problem and end the story.
Suddenly, he saw his mother and brother down below.
Now the story is starting to come down.
George scrambled down the tree and gave his mother a big hug. The end.
Now the problem is solved and the story is back down where we started.

- Explain that you will be giving students time to practice writing both walking stories and climbing stories. Relate writing with reading that you do in class:

We will also be noticing these different kinds of stories when we read.

Lesson: Introducing Poetry

- To introduce poetry and discuss the difference between a story and a poem: copy a short poem onto a chart stand, whiteboard, or interactive whiteboard.
- Ask students to read it and discuss with a partner if it is a climbing story or walking story (neither; it's a poem).
- Explain that sometimes a poem can tell a story and other times it can describe something.

- Ask students:

  What is a poem? How can you tell if writing on a page is a poem or a story? (looks different: shorter lines, more white spaces; sounds different: rhythm, repetition, sometimes rhyme)

- Explain that, along with writing climbing and walking stories, students will also be writing poetry.

Walking Story Strips

Name: _____

Title: _____

_____	_____	_____	_____
_____	_____	_____	_____
_____	_____	_____	_____
_____	_____	_____	_____

Name: _____

Title: _____

_____	_____	_____	_____
_____	_____	_____	_____
_____	_____	_____	_____
_____	_____	_____	_____

Pembroke Publishers ©2011 *Writing Power* by Adrienne Gear ISBN 978-1-55138-263-0

Climbing Story Strip

Name: _____

Title: _____

Pembroke Publishers ©2011 *Writing Power* by Adrienne Gear ISBN 978-1-55138-263-0

6 Technical Power: Tools for Writing

Throughout this book, several writing techniques are introduced. These techniques are used to support and enhance student writing. Techniques can be introduced to the students in a mini-lesson, then applied and practiced during specific writing lessons so that students become familiar with them. The goal is that students apply them independently as they write. Teachers can create an anchor chart of Writing Techniques in their classroom. As each new technique is introduced, it can be added and used as a reference when students are writing.

The following is a list of writing technique lessons included in this chapter:

- Adding Details
- Similes
- Anchor Lines
- Voice
- Six Senses
- Vocabulary
- Writing in the Third Person
- Personification
- First Impressions
- Dialogue

P = primary
I = intermediate

This list includes books about writing or being a writer that can enhance your lessons on writing technique and help you acknowledge and celebrate the craft of writing in your classroom.

Lesson: Introducing Writing Techniques

Books about Writing, Becoming a Writer, Writing Techniques

Mary Jane Auch, *The Plot Chickens* (I)

Kate Banks, *Max's Words* (P, I)

Eileen Christelow, *What Do Authors Do?* (P)

Kate Duke, *Aunt Isabel Tells A Good One* (P, I)

Mordecai Gernstein, *A BOOK* (I)

Esther Hershenhorn, *S is for Story: A Writer's Alphabet* (P, I)

Barbara Kanninen, *A Story With Pictures* (P)

Helen Lester, *Author: A True Story* (P, I)

Gail Carson Levine, *Writing Magic: Creating Stories That Fly* (I)

Nancy Loewen, *The Writer's Toolbox* (I)

Patricia McLaughlin, *Word After Word After Word* (P, I)

Joan Lowery Nixon, *If You Were a Writer* (I)

Josephine Nobisso, *Show, Don't Tell: The Secrets of Writing* (I)

Kevin O'Malley, *Once Upon a Motorcycle Dude* (I)

Kevin O'Malley, *Once Upon a Royal Superbaby* (I)

Roni Schotter, *The Boy Who Loved Words* (P, I)

Roni Schotter, *Nothing Ever Happens on 90th Street* (P)

Eileen Spinelli, *The Best Story* (P, I)

Mélanie Watt, *Chester's Masterpiece* (P)

Prior to the specific technique lessons, you might want to introduce the concept of writing techniques to your students.

- Begin the lesson:

  When a hockey player is learning to play hockey or a ballet dancer is learning to dance, they don't just tie up their skates or ballet shoes and go for it. To become good at sports or dance or anything, you need to learn the skills and techniques, and then you need to practice them over and over. It's the same with writing. Writers don't just pick up a pencil and start writing. They need to learn skills and techniques, and then they need to practice them.

- Brainstorm what techniques a hockey player might need to learn (skating, shooting, stick handling, passing). Brainstorm ballet techniques (feet positions, arm positions, barre exercises, plié, arabesque).
- Ask students what techniques a writer might need to learn.
- Explain that you will be teaching them new writing techniques and that they will be getting lots of opportunities to practice them. These techniques will help them become better and more skilful writers.

Lesson: Adding Details

Many of us have experienced student writing that sounds robotic. Years of journal writing have produced students who simply list events of their day-to-day lives in "bed-to-bed" stories: *I woke up… I did this… I did that… I did this… I did that… then I went to bed.* Teaching students to *write a fact, then add a detail* can help them to just say "No" to robot writing.

- Begin the lesson:

  Writers have an important job. Their job is to keep their readers interested in what they have to say. Writers want their readers to keep on reading—not to read a few sentences, yawn, and put the book down. As writers, we want to make sure that our readers stay interested and keep on reading. So we need to make sure our writing is interesting, not boring.

- Write the following examples on the board and discuss the difference:

  Example 1:
  I love snow. (general statement: a lot of people could say this)

  I love snow. When it snows I always do a "snow dance" in the kitchen! (Adding a detail after a fact makes the writing more interesting to read)

  Example 2:
  I am a soccer player. I am a student. I have brother. (This is robot writing because it feels like you are reading out a list)

  I am a soccer player. I play for the West Coast Ravens and this year we're going to win the Cup! (Writing a fact plus an example or detail makes the writing more interesting)

- Read and discuss the following examples:

  Example 1:
  My name is Cassandra. I'm eleven years old. I have reddish-brown hair. I have pale skin and freckles. I have bluish-green eyes. I like to swim. I'm afraid of sharks.

  Example 2:
  My name is Cassandra. I am eleven years old. I have hair the color of cinnamon toast (without the crust), fair skin, except where it's speckled like an overripe banana. My eyes are like summer mountains (that's blue with a little bit of green, in case you were wondering). I like to swim in anything except the ocean because I'm scared that a shark will bite my leg off. My mum says that sharks only swim in very warm water but I don't believe her.

- In partners, have students discuss which passage they found more interesting and engaging, and why. Explain that Example 1 is more like a list, or robot writing.

  It's not very interesting because there are no interesting details—it's just a list. The second one is much more interesting to read because, even though the writer told us the same thing, she added a lot of personal details, voice, and similes to make the writing unique.

  Good writers don't just write "lists"—for every fact they write, they try to add a detail or an example so that the reader feels that they are sharing something personal with them and not just listing a lot of general facts.

This story strip by a Grade 2 student is an example of robot writing.

Lesson: Similes

Books Built on Similes

Anthony Browne, *My Dad* (P)
Anthony Browne, *My Mum* (P)
Loreen Leedy, *Crazy Like a Fox: A Simile Story* (P, I)
Hanoch Piven, *My Dog is as Smelly As Dirty Socks* (P, I)
Hanoch Piven, *My Best Friend Is As Sharp as a Pencil* (P, I)

Patricia McLaughlin, *Night Noises* (P, I)
Patricia McLaughlin, *All the Places to Love* (P, I)
Cynthia Rylant, *Snow* (P, I)
Audrey Wood, *Quick as a Cricket* (P)
Jane Yolen, *Owl Moon* (I)

• Begin the lesson with some examples of similes on the board/whiteboard/ overhead:

Teacher Model

> *He crept into the room as quiet as a mouse*
> *The cloud was fluffy like cotton candy*
> *He was as angry as a grizzly bear*
> *The snowflake sparkled like millions of tiny diamonds*
> *Her skin was as soft as velvet*

Ask students what they notice that the sentences have in common.

• Explain to the students they will be learning a technique that is often used by writers.

This technique is called *simile*, and it is a way of describing by comparing two things that aren't really alike. Similes connect these two things with either the word "as" or the word "like." Similes can help readers make connections and visualize.
There are some similes that are well-known or common, but have been overused.
(you may want to introduce the term "cliché")

> *Wise as an owl*
> *Busy as a bee*
> *As cold as ice*

Encourage students to try to create original and surprising similes.

• Pass out the Simile and You Will See! sheet (page 54). Explain to students that they are going to try to create some similes. The chart has two spaces beside each prompt: one for a common simile and one for an original.

Once students are familiar with this writing technique, invite them to listen for similes when you are reading aloud. Primary students can give a thumbs-up whenever they hear a simile being read.

• Remind the students that, when you create a simile, the two things you are comparing are different but share something in common. Discuss with your students why the examples below don't really work (because the adjective or describing word does not really match the noun).

> *As crunchy as a volcano.*
> *As silly as a spider.*
> *Friendly like a mushroom.*
> *Crazy like peanut butter.*

These samples of similes are by students in Grade 4 (Simile and You Will See! sheet) and Grade 3 (list of similes).

Name: _____

Simile and You Will See!

As cold as...	ice	A popsicle in the freezer for a year
Hot like...	sun	the burning core of the earth
As brave as...	football player	as brave as a knight that tames a dragon
Slow like...	slug	As slow as my sister in the morning!
As fast as...	athletes	fire on dry grass
Quiet like...	a mouse	a muted T.V.
As angry as...	a lion	Hitler before the war
As funny as...	a circus trainer	Americas home videos
Annoying like...	ooing dang doing a monkey reapeating sound	my sister whining

I'm as pretty as a flower.
I'm as clean as glass.
I'm as talented as a musicon.
I'm as nice as a butterfly.
I'm as fast as a puma.
As blue as the sky.
As bright as the sun.

Lesson: Anchor Lines

Books that Include Anchor Lines

Anthony Browne, *My Dad* (P)
Anthony Browne, *My Mum* (P)

Judith Viorst, *Alexander and the Terrible, Horrible, No Good, Very Bad Day* (P, I)

For more on walking stories, see page 36.

- Draw a picture of an anchor on the board. Ask the students:

  What is it? (an anchor).
  What is it used for? (to hold a ship steady and to keep it from drifting away).

  Explain that sometimes writers use anchors to hold their writing steady. An anchor line is a sentence or phrase that a writer repeats throughout a piece of writing. Often, anchor lines are used in walking stories.

  The repeated line helps connect the details of the story to the topic.

- Read several books and ask students to listen for the anchor lines. Tell students that they will be learning to use anchor lines in many of the writing lessons that they will be doing.

Lesson: Six Senses

- Begin the lesson:

  As good writers know, writing isn't just describing things for our readers to see, but about inviting our readers to use all their senses when they are reading. Including all the senses in our writing can really help engage our readers and make the writing come alive for them.

- Brainstorm six senses: sight, sound, taste, smell, touch, and feeling (emotion). Write the word *taste* on the board. Begin modeling words to describe how something might taste: sour, sweet, delicious, bitter, horrible, tangy, tasty, grainy, stale, fresh, chewy, slippery, soft, crunchy, mouth-watering, syrupy, spicy, etc. Invite students to participate in the brainstorming.
- Divide your class into six groups. Give each group a chart paper. (Prior to the lesson, print one of the six senses words on the top of each chart paper. Include a visual if you wish.) Explain that they will have one minute to brainstorm as many words as they can to describe the sense printed at the top of their paper.
- When time is up, the chart papers are passed clockwise to the next group. Upon receiving a new chart (new sense), the groups must read over the words that are already there and begin to add new words. The rotation continues until each group has had a turn with each chart. This becomes more challenging as the lists become longer, so allow more time for each rotation.
- When the groups are finished, the anchor charts can be displayed in the room and referred to during other writing lessons.

I recommend making anchor charts for your classroom by rewriting these lists in large, neat printing and with correct spelling, because students will be referring to them when they write.

Lesson: Voice

Books with Great Voice

Jamie Lee Curtis, *Today I Feel Silly* (P)
Kevin Henkes, *Lily's Purple Plastic Purse* (P, I)
Anne Hoffman, *Amazing Grace* (I)

Karen Hoffman, *I Wanna Iguana* (P, I)
Barbara Joosse, *Please is a Good Thing to Say* (P, I)

- Begin the lesson:

  Some writers do an excellent job of making their characters seem real. One way to do this is to give the character a voice. When you write with voice, your readers feel like you are talking right to them and it helps them get to know you, or the character you are writing about, much better. Let's have a look at writing samples. One of these samples makes good use of voice and the other doesn't. See if you can decide which is which.

  Example 1:
  I am Jack. I have dark hair and brown eyes. Hockey is my favorite sport. I am learning how to play the drums but I'm not very good. I have a big sister and a little brother.

  Example 2:
  My name is Jack but everyone calls me JJ. Don't ask me why because my last name is Renny. I have brown eyes and hair that is trying to be black but didn't quite make it. Hockey is the most awesomest sport in the world and anyone who doesn't like it shouldn't be allowed to live. I am learning to play the drums but my mom would probably tell you that I'm not very good yet. I am a middle child—which is a nice way of saying that I have a bossy big sister and a tag-along baby brother.

- Have students discuss these examples in partners. Which example has voice? Which one is more interesting to read? Why? What are some specific examples of voice in the more-interesting example?
- Explain that good writers don't just tell about a character, but they also try to create characters who seem real and have real personalities.
- Ask students to help you give voice to the following sentences

  Jonathan's favorite drink was 7-Up.
  My teacher gives me too much homework.
  My sister sometimes bugs me.

- Explain that students will be getting time to practice adding voice to their writing in several of the upcoming writing lessons.

Lesson: Vocabulary and Triple-Scoop Words

Books about Words and Vocabulary

Kate Banks, *Max's Words* (P, I)
Debra Frasier, *Miss Alainius: A Vocabulary Disaster* (P, I)

Jane O'Conner, *Fancy Nancy* (P)
Roni Schotter, *The Boy Who Loved Words* (P, I)

"The difference between the right word and the almost right word is the difference between lightning and a lightning bug."
—Mark Twain.

- Begin the lesson:

An artist starts with a blank canvas and creates an image by mixing the paint and carefully spreading and arranging the paint on the canvas. A writer is like an artist. The only difference is that a writer starts with a blank page instead of a canvas and uses words instead of paint to create images. Good writers carefully choose, arrange, and rearrange their words because they want their readers to be able to see the story in their minds. There are approximately a quarter of a million words in the English language—that's a lot of words to choose from! Artists spend a long time mixing colors until they find just the right tone. Writers need to take time to find the right words, the best words. There are so many ordinary and plain words—I call them the single-scoop words, because they are just like one scoop of ice cream. The single scoop is okay, but most often it leaves you wishing you had more. But there are also many amazing words that we can use when we write—I call these triple-scoop words—delicious words that make you feel full and satisfied.

Writers need a lot of words in order to make their writing interesting, just like an artist needs lots of colors to make a painting interesting. If an artist used the same two colors all the time, the pictures would be boring to look at. If a writer used the same words over and over, the writing would be boring to read. Having a huge palette of words can help us become more colorful writers.

On this chart I have written a few single-scoop words. Who can help me turn them into triple-scoopers?

Single Scoop	Triple Scoop
sad	devastated, depressed
mad	furious, livid
good	amazing, fantastic

- Invite students to brainstorm words for the chart:
- Once the students have the idea, pass out the Triple-Scoop Word chart (page 55). Students can work to complete this chart either with a partner or independently. This sheet can be kept inside their writing notebooks to refer to when they are editing, changing, or rearranging words.

Lesson: Writing in the Third Person

- Begin the lesson:

Writers often get ideas for their writing from their own memories and experiences. But sometimes when they write about these experiences, they change the story to sound like it is not really about them but about someone else. A writer might create a character based on him- or herself, or someone they know, but change the story so it is not being told as if the writer was talking about him- or herself. Today we are going to write using this writing technique. It's called writing in the third person.

- Write the following sentences on the board or chart paper:

  I didn't want to go with them because I felt too nervous. (first person)
  She didn't want to go with them because she felt too nervous. (third person)

  Ask students to read the two sentences and discuss what is different about them. Explain the difference between first person and third person.

  First-person writing is when the writer is the one who is telling the story. This is sometimes called a personal narrative because the person writing is narrating or telling the story. Third-person writing sounds as if a person outside the story, or narrator, is telling the story.

  Explain that it's an easy technique, but can be a very effective way to change the voice of writing.

- Students can practice changing from first to third person using a previous writing piece. You could also use this writing technique as a focus for any lesson.

  Today, even though you are writing about a feeling you have experienced, I want you to try to write about it in third person, as if it actually happened to someone else. Next time you are reading a book, think about whether the writer wrote the story in the first person or the third person.

Lesson: Personification

- Write the word *personification* on the board. Explain that the writing technique for this lesson is called personification. Ask students if they can identify a smaller word within the word on the board that might help them figure out the meaning. Underline or circle *person*. Explain that the word "person" is a good way to remember this technique.

  Personification is when writers write about an object as if it were a person—in other words, they add human qualities to an inanimate (not alive) object. What do you think human qualities might be? What makes a human different from a rock, for example? (movement/action, thoughts and feelings, voice) Creating inanimate objects that are able to think, feel, and act the same as a human can be a helpful way for a reader to understand your writing better.

- Model a few examples and discuss the use of personification:

Teacher Model

> The *flowers begged* for water.
> The *wind screamed* as it raced around the house.
> The *house was lazy* and unkempt.
> *Lightning danced* across the sky.
> *Trees bowed* to the ground.
> The carved *pumpkin smiled* at me.
> The *vines wove their thin fingers* around the tree trunk
> The *wind whispered* softly in the night.
> The *stars winked* at me.

- Have students make a T-chart on a blank paper or use the Personification Match organizer on page 56. On one side, students list several inanimate objects. Objects in nature work the best: e.g., stars, cloud, leaf, ocean, grass, etc. On the other side, students list action words (verbs)— anything a human can do with their hands, feet, and mouth; e.g., jump, scratch, whisper.
- When both sides of the chart are complete, model how to match up a word from one side with a word on the other. Encourage students to create unique and unusual images, avoiding ones that they may have already heard before: e.g., *the leaves whispered* has already been used; *the leaves tiptoed* is new.
- Once students have matched up all their words, invite them to choose their three best matches and expand them into a sentence. Model how to expand by adding an adverb (to indicate *how*) and a noun (to indicate *where*). Example: *leaves dance* becomes *The leaves dance quietly across the frosty ground.*

Lesson: First Impressions

Anchor Books for First Impressions

Barbara Abercrombie, *Charlie Anderson* (P, I)
Mac Barnett, *Billy Twitters and his Blue Whale Problem* (P)
Anthony Browne, *Willy the Wizard* (P, I)
Paulette Bourgeois, *Franklin in the Dark* (P)
Laurel Croza, *I Know Here* (I)
Jennifer Riesmeyer Elvgren, *Josias, Hold the Book* (I)
Marie Hall Ets, *Gilberto and the Wind* (P, I)
Greg Foley, *Willoughby and the Lion* (P, I)
Norton Juster, *The Hello, Good-bye Window* (P, I)
Olivier Ka, *My Great Big Mama* (P, I)

Eric Litwin, *Pete the Cat* (P)
Peter H. Reynolds, *Ish* (P, I)
Chris Raschka, *Little Black Crow* (P)
Eric Rohmann, *Clara and Asha* (P, I)
Danielle Simard, *The Little Word Catcher* (P, I)
Lane Smith, *It's a Book* (I)
Kathy Stinson, *Mom and Dad Don't Live Together Anymore* (P, I)
Ferida Wolff, *It Is the Wind* (P)
Audrey Wood, *Sweet Dream Pie* (P, I)
Wong Herbert Yee, *Who Likes Rain?* (P, I)

- Write *first impression* on the board. Ask students what it means. Ask for some examples of situations in which they need to make a good first impression (a job interview, first day at a new school, first time over at a friend's house). Ask students what they might do to make a good first impression (good manners, eye contact, shake hands).

  These are important tips or techniques that we would use to ensure that we make a good first impression.

- Ask students why first impressions are important (because it makes the other person want to get to know you). Explain that writers also need to make a good first impression on their readers. Ask the students why writers might need to do this (so that the reader becomes interested and engaged, and wants to continue reading).

  Writer's have their own set of techniques to make a good first impressions on their readers.

- Share the opening sentences of the anchor books with students. Invite students to read them and to think about what writing techniques were used.

Start with a problem:
Willy the Wizard by Anthony Browne
Franklin in the Dark by Paulette Bourgeois
Josias, Hold the Book by Jennifer Riesmeyer Elvgren
Start with dialogue:
I Know Here by Laurel Croza
Billy Twitters and his Blue Whale Problem by Mac Barnett
Clara and Asha by Eric Rohmann
It's a Book by Lane Smith
Start with a statement or fact:
The Hello, Good-bye Window by Norton Juster
Mom and Dad Don't Live Together Anymore by Kathy Stinson
My Great Big Mama by Olivier Ka
Willoughby and the Lion by Greg Folley
Ish by Peter H. Reynolds
Start with a question:
The Little Word Catcher by Danielle Simard
Little Black Crow by Chris Raschka
It Is the Wind by Ferida Wolff
Start with an action:
Charlie Anderson by Barbara Abercrombie
Sweet Dream Pie by Audrey Wood
Pete the Cat by Eric Litwin
Start with a sound:
Gilberto and the Wind by Marie Hall Ets
Who Likes Rain? by Wong Herbert Yee

- Discuss and create an anchor chart for your classroom:

  How to Make a Good First Impression
  A good writer can begin a story with
  - a problem
  - dialogue or conversation
  - a simple statement or fact
  - a question
  - an action
  - a sound

- Use Making a Good First Impression on page 57 to have students write their own story starters.

Lesson: Dialogue

- Begin the lesson:

  One of the main differences between story-writing and information-writing is the characters. Stories have characters who experience things, feel things, and often say things to other characters. When characters in a story are talking, it is called *dialogue*. Dialogue helps readers to get to know the characters better and almost feel that they are inside the story, listening in on the characters as they talk.

While there are many grammar books that include isolated exercises on dialogue, I prefer to have students practice in the context of their writing. Several lessons in this book will include dialogue as a writing technique.

Dialogue is also a nice way for a writer to give the reader a break from reading longer descriptive passages. When a writer is including dialogue, there are three important rules to follow.

Rule 1: A New Line Every Time! Every time a new person is speaking you must start writing on a new line.

Rule 2: Surround Sound! Quotation marks must be used to surround the sound of the character speaking.

Rule 3: P.B.Q. (Punctuation Before Quotations)! Any punctuation—including commas, periods, question marks, or exclamation marks—must be included before the closing quotation mark (unless the question mark or exclamation mark belong with the sentence outside the quotation).

Write the following sentences on the board and invite students to help you show the dialogue correctly, following the rules. Talk through the rules as you write.

Teacher Model

Example without quotes:
I don't like green bananas the monkey said. Why not? asked his mother. Because they taste like glue the monkey replied. How do you know what glue tastes like? his mother asked. Just do said the monkey.

Example with quotes:
"I don't like green bananas," the monkey said.
"Why not?" asked his mother.
"Because they taste like glue," the monkey replied
"How do you know what glue tastes like?" his mother asked.
"Just do," said the monkey.

• Remind students that dialogue is an important and interesting addition to a story. Encourage them to try to include it in their next writing piece.

Simile and You Will See!

Name: _____

As cold as…	*snow*	*my fingertips when my ski gloves get wet*
Hot like…		
As brave as…		
Slow like…		
As fast as…		
Quiet like…		
As angry as…		
As funny as…		
Annoying like…		
As boring as…		
Loud like…		
As soft as…		
Rough like…		
As black as…		
White like …		
As loud as…		

A simile is _____

_____

Pembroke Publishers ©2011 *Writing Power* by Adrienne Gear ISBN 978-1-55138-263-0

Triple-Scoop Word Chart

Name: _____

Single Scoop	Triple Scoop
hot	*sweltering, melting, scorching, roasting*
cold	
wet	
fun	
good	
bad	
tired	
hungry	
sad	
happy	
mad	
pretty	
big	
small	
said	
nice	

Pembroke Publishers ©2011 *Writing Power* by Adrienne Gear ISBN 978-1-55138-263-0

Personification Match

Name: _____

Inanimate Object (something that is not alive)	Action you can do with your hands, feet, or mouth

- Now draw a line to match up one word from the left column with one word from the right. Try to match two words to create a surprising or unique combination.
- Choose your best two matches. Put a star beside them. Write them below and expand them by adding a *how* (adverb) and a *where* (a place).

Example: *leaves dance* can become *The leaves dance quietly across the park.*

_____

_____

Making a Good First Impression

Name: _____

Now it's your turn to make a great first impression!

Start with a simple statement:

_____

_____

Start with someone speaking or a conversation:

_____

_____

Start with a problem:

_____

_____

Start with an action:

_____

_____

Start with a question:

_____

_____

Start with a sound:

_____

_____

Now choose one of your story starters and continue writing. See if your first impression turns into a great story!

Pembroke Publishers ©2011 *Writing Power* by Adrienne Gear ISBN 978-1-55138-263-0

Writing Power Lessons

The Writing Power Song
(to the tune of Old Macdonald)

When I write, I do invite
My readers all to think.
The words I write are gifts to you.
This page will be our link.
With some thinking here, and some
    thinking there,
Thinking here, thinking there
Thinking, thinking everywhere!
When I write, I do invite
My readers all to think!

When I write, I do invite
My readers to connect
To things you've done or things you've
    seen.
That's what you can expect!
Some connecting here, connecting
    there,
Connections here, connections there
There are connections everywhere!
When I write, I do invite
My readers to connect!

When I write, I do invite
Some visualizing please.
I paint a picture with my words.
You visualize with ease.
A word down here makes a picture
    there,
(point to "a book" and then to your
    head)
Word here, picture there
Thinking pictures everywhere!
When I write, I do invite
Some visualizing please!

When I write I do invite
A question from your head.
Your thinking wheels begin to turn
From something that you read.
With some wondering here, wonder-
    ing there,
Here a wonder, there a wonder
Everywhere a WONDER!
When I write, I do invite
A question from your head!

When I write, I do invite
My readers to infer.
I might not tell you everything.
You might not know for sure.
Add a maybe here and a maybe there,
Here a may, there a be,
Everywhere a maybe!
When I write, I do invite
my readers to infer!

When I write I do invite
My readers' thoughts to change.
You read this part and suddenly
Your thoughts get rearranged.
With an "ah-ha" here and an "ah-ha"
    there,
"Ah!" here, "ha!" there,
Transformed thinking everywhere!
When I write I do invite
My reader's thoughts to change!

Repeat Verse 1

7 Inviting Readers to Connect

Making connections to the books we read enhances understanding. A story becomes more meaningful when it triggers memories of similar experiences, feelings, people, or places from within our own lives. Information makes more sense when we can connect it to something we already know and understand. Any text, whether it be a story or information, is understood more deeply when it is read in terms of our own experience and knowledge. When a chapter of our own life story becomes woven through the fabric of the text we are reading, when we feel what the character feels or experience what the character experiences, the story we're reading becomes our story too. Connecting can be the simplest yet most profound way to enhance understanding.

When teaching this reading strategy to students, I explain that connecting is when the story you are reading and the story of your own life come together:

> Your life is a story, it's just not written down on paper. Every experience you have in your life adds a chapter to your life story. When you read, sometimes something in the story will trigger a memory, tug on a heartstring, remind you of a place you've been, a person you knew, a feeling you've had.

As writers, we need to strive to find ways to invite readers to make those connections. One way to support these connections is by choosing writing topics that our readers will most easily connect to: feelings, family, friendship and school experiences, to name a few. We write about the stories of our own lives in the hope that our readers will connect to theirs.

Thinking Power to Connect

For the lessons in this chapter, students are encouraged to use the "chapters" from their Memory Pockets to find ideas for their writing. Teachers are also encouraged to model their own writing, using personal memories and experiences. Writing techniques are introduced and practiced throughout a series of lessons. While it is not essential, it is strongly recommended that the writing lessons coincide with your reading focus and instructions on making connections while reading. This way, students begin to recognize the power of connecting both through reading and writing.

Connecting to Me

Anchor Books for Connecting to Me

Karen Beaumont, *I Like Myself* (P)
Nancy Carlson, *I Like Me* (P)
Wendy Ewald, *The Best Part of Me* (P, I)
Walter Dean Myers, *Looking Like Me* (I)

Allia Zobel Nolan, *What I Like About Me!* (P)
Marianne Richmond, *Hurray for You! A Celebration of You-ness* (P)

Narrative Power: Walking Story

Technical Power: Adding Details (p. 43); Voice (p. 48)

Lesson 1: Planning

- Write the following statements on the board: *Good readers make connections while they read. These connections can help them understand the book better.* Ask students:

Who can tell me what a connection is? (when something in the book reminds us of something that happened to us before). Knowing that readers make connections when they read can help us become better writers. Good writers want their readers to make connections to their writing. If we look at our Brain Pockets, which pocket do you think we may be focusing on when we write "connect" writing? (Memory Pocket) What sort of memories or experiences do you think we could use for writing that our readers might connect to? (memories of family, school, friends, etc.)

- Explain to students that you have brought some picture books to share. Show the books and read the titles. Ask the students:

What do you notice that these books have in common? (They all focus on "me" and what makes us unique and special) Readers will connect to these books because they will be able to see things in these characters that remind them of themselves. Good writers want their readers to connect. Writing about ourselves and what makes us unique helps our readers to think about themselves and what makes them unique.

- Model a Me Web on a chart paper or the interactive whiteboard, filling in words describing three areas of Me: *Who I Am*; *What I Look Like*; *How I Act*. Remind students as you model that you are trying to include specific details that make "me" unique. Have students turn and share two ideas for each part of the web with a partner.
- Pass out the Connecting to Me Planning Sheet (page 75). Have students work independently on their planning sheets.

Lesson 2: Writing

- Remind students:

Good readers make connections when they read. Good writers help their readers to make these connections.

- Explain to students that they will be using the ideas from their Connecting to Me Planning Sheets to write a piece about "me."
- Begin by modeling your own writing:

> I like me! I have blue eyes and light brown hair. I have skinny arms like a monkey. Sometimes my boys call me "Monkey Mom!" I am a mother of two and a teacher to many. I am a hockey mom: "Great save, Oliver!" "Nice pass, Spencer!" I love snow. When it snows I do a snow dance in the kitchen! I like to be with my friends: "How have you been?" I also like quiet times just with me. I am determined: "Don't give up! You can do it!" I am hardworking and I think a lot—sometimes my brain is so busy that I wish I had an Off button! But at the end of the day, I am the only me I have—and I like that! I like me!

- After sharing your writing, ask students what they noticed about your writing. What did they like? Remind students that when they begin to write they should try to add details and examples to make their writing interesting instead of simply writing a list—no robot writing allowed! Explain that using their planning web can help them organize their ideas for writing. Each "arm" of the web is one big idea, but can be expanded with details and examples.

Lesson 3: Conferencing and Editing for All Invitations to Connect

With a partner, students can share their writing. Remind them to share a connection they made to their partner's writing as well as a "star" and a "wish" (see page 18). After conferencing, students can use either the 3, 2, 1…Edit! or 1, 2, 3, 4—Edit! (page 20) checklist to help them edit their piece. You can conduct individual conferences during this time: I try to meet individually with two or three students per week. (See page 23 for Writing Power Conference Record.)

Lesson 4: Publishing and Sharing for All Invitations to Connect

Students can develop a published copy. Choose two or three students to read their pieces aloud to the class. Some students who complete their writing early might wish to add an illustration to their work.

Story Strip for Emergent Writers: Me

Emergent writers can create a story strip about "Me" with the following criteria provided:

I like me (picture and who you are)	I like… (picture and word, then add a detail)	I am good at… (picture and word, then add a detail)	I can… (picture and descriptor)

I still use Donald Graves' Author's Chair idea (Graves, 1978) when students are sharing their writing with the class. A simple sign with the words *Author's Chair* (or *Writer's Chair*) hung on the back of a chair helps the reader to feel recognized as an authentic writer.

This story strip is by a student in Grade 1.

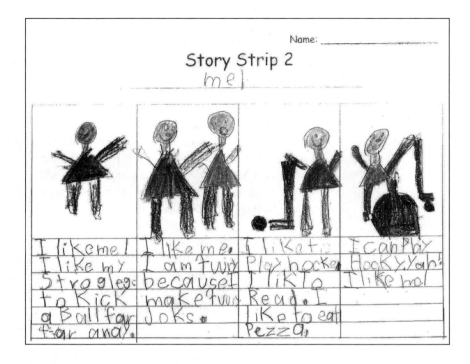

Name: _____

Story Strip 2

me!

I like me! I like my strog legs to kick a Ball far far away.

I like me. I am fun because I make fun Joks.

I like to Play hocke I like to Read. I like to eat Pezza.

I can Play Hocky yah! I like me!

Connecting to Feelings

Anchor Books for Connecting to Feelings

Aliki, *Feelings* (P, I)
Janan Cain, *The Way I Feel* (P, I)
Vicki Churchill, *Sometimes I Like to Curl Up in a Ball* (P)
Jamie Lee Curtis, *Today I Feel Silly* (P)

Florence Parry Heide, *Some Things Are Scary* (I)
Todd Parr, *The Feelings Book* (P)
Todd Parr, *The Feel Good Book* (P)
Dr. Seuss, *My Many Colored Days* (P, I)

Narrative Power: Walking Story (primary) or Climbing Story

Technical Power: Adding Details (p. 43); Similes (p. 45); Voice (p. 47)

Lesson 1: Planning

- Remind students that you are working on writing that invites readers to make connections. Show/share the title of several of the suggested anchor books. Ask students what they have in common (they are books about feelings). Ask students why "feeling" books might be ones that readers would make connections to (because everyone has feelings so everyone can make connections). Read one of the books aloud.
- Brainstorm a list of feelings words down the left side of a chart paper. I find it helpful to separate feelings into positive and negative (see below).

Positive Feelings	Negative Feelings
Proud, excited, happy, loved, silly, grateful, great, relaxed, content, brave, lucky,	Sad, angry, jealous, mad, furious, disappointed, frustrated, embarrassed, annoyed, scared, nervous, worried

- Ask students to choose one of the feelings words from the list. Invite them to go into their Memory Pocket and think about a time in their life when they felt this way.

- Model a few examples, then call on students to share theirs.

Teacher Model

I felt sad once when my friend stopped talking to me for no reason.
I felt scared once when I thought the shadow in the hall I could see from my bed was a robber.
I felt excited when my team scored in overtime and won the game.
I feel frustrated when I can't find the Lego piece that I need to make my Star Wars ship.
I feel nervous when I have to stand up in front of the class to give a speech.

- Pass out the Connecting to Feelings Planning Sheet (see page 76). Students can complete the sheets by searching their Memory Pockets to think of ideas for each of the feelings.

Lesson 2: Writing

- Remind students that their writing focus this week is connecting to feelings. Explain that they will be choosing one of their feelings examples from their Connecting to Feelings Planning Sheet to develop into a piece of writing.
- Model your example:

Teacher Model

The feelings word I chose was *disappointed*. I felt disappointed when the Canucks didn't win the Stanley Cup.

When Sophie Gets Angry…Really, Really Angry by Molly Bang provides a good example of how to develop a piece with a focus on one emotion.

- Have students share a connection they made to the teacher model with a partner. Students can then revisit their completed Connecting to Feelings Planning Sheet and select one feeling they would like to use for their writing. Before writing, have them share with a partner which feelings word they will be writing about.
- Explain that, when they are writing, they will need to include the *who, what, where, when,* and *why* so that their readers will understand how they came to have that feeling.

Lessons 3 and 4

See page 61.

Story Strip for Emergent Writers: Feelings

See page 65 for a sample Story Strip: Feelings.

I feel happy when… Include detail and voice	I feel sad when… Include detail and voice	I feel excited when… Include detail and voice	I feel shy when… Include detail and voice

This Connecting to Feelings sample is by a student in Grade 2.

the ~~big~~ humungus loss

tonite is the night tonite the Canuks are going to win the Stanly cup. they are goin to beet the Bostan Bruins in game 7 be the frst team in frenchifchiz histre to be Stanly cup champs. Ruin the Bruins my dad sez. Are frends came over and we lots of food. My sister and my dad wor ther jerzez. I have a tatoo on my cheek. We wer waving the flags. We stud up and sang O Canada with the nice fat giy so loud. The puk dropt. After abut 5 minutes it went bad so bad. The Bruins keep scoring 1-2-3-4. 4-0.

IT was over - we lost the cup. My disappointment was so big it fills my hole body. I cryd into my Canuks pillow until I fell asleep.

the end

This story strip is by a Grade 1 student.

Connecting to a Special Grown-Up

Anchor Books for Connecting to a Special Grown-Up

Anthony Browne, *My Dad* (P)
Anthony Browne, *My Mum* (P)
Nick Butterworth, *My Grandpa is Amazing* (P)
Gaby Goldsacks, *My Mom is Great* (P)
Mercer Mayer, *Just Me and My Dad* (P)
Sally Morgan, *Me and My Dad* (P, I)
Carl Norac, *My Daddy is a Giant* (P, I)

Carl Norac, *My Grandpa is a Champion* (P, I)
Carl Norac, *My Grandma is a Star* (P, I)
Joanne Ryder, *My Father's Hands* (P, I)
Joanne Ryder, *My Mother's Voice* (P, I)
Ashley Wolff, *I Call My Grandpa Papa* (P, I)
Ashley Wolff, *I Call My Grandma Nana* (P, I)

Narrative Power: Walking Story

Technical Power: Adding Detail (p. 43); Similes (p. 45); Anchor Lines (p. 47)

Lesson 1: Planning

- Remind students that they are working on writing that invites readers to make connections. Previous writing has included connecting to self and connecting to feelings. This week they will be focusing on connections to something new.
- Share one or two of the suggested anchor books, or pass copies of different examples to small groups. Discuss what these books have in common (all books are about a parent or special grown-up). Ask what connections students were making when they read them. Ask students what else they noticed in their reading (personal details, repeated lines).
- Explain that the next writing piece will focus on a special grown-up. It can be a parent, a grandparent, an aunt or uncle, or a friend. Ask students to choose

a person they know and love very much. Ask the students to share with a partner:

- Who their special grown-up is
- One interesting thing about this person
- A special memory (from their Memory Pocket) about this person
- A feeling they get when they think about this person

- Pass out the Connecting to a Special Grown-Up Planning Sheet (pages 77 and 78, copied double-sided) and invite students to complete it. If there is time, they can share ideas with a partner.

Lesson 2: Writing

- Remind students:

Good readers make connections when they read. Good writers help their readers to make these connections.

- Explain to students that they will be using the ideas from their planning sheets to write a piece about their special grown-up.

We hope when our readers read our writing, they will make connections to their own special grown-up.

- Model your writing:

Teacher Model

My Grannie is lovely. She was born far away in England and lived through the war. She has soft ginger hair and a lovely voice. She hums songs from the Sound of Music *when she knits her little baby blanket squares. When she looks at the mountains she says, "Just look at my mountains! Aren't they LUV-ER-LY!" My Grannie is lovely. My Grannie makes me laugh when she tries to skip with a skipping rope because she can't really skip. She always says, "Oh, dear – the rope is broken!" My Grannie is lovely. My Grannie makes delicious beef barley soup and shortbread that melts in your mouth. My Grannie's hands are always cold. "Cold hands, warm heart," she always says. And she's right. My Grannie is lovely.*

- Ask students what writing techniques they noticed about this piece (adding details, anchor lines, similes). Encourage the students to include an anchor line and similes when they are describing their special grown-up, as well as to add details that make their writing different from anyone else's.

Lessons 3 and 4

See page 61.

Story Strip for Emergent Writers: My Special Grown-Up

See page 68 for a sample Story Strip: My Special Grown-Up.

My _____ is...	My _____ can...	One day, my _____ and I ...	I love my_____ because ...

This sample is by a Grade 4 student.

My Dad is Special!
He was Born in Hong Kong, China.
His hobbies are playing poker and
M.J., he is a biker and a terrific
builder. Did you know that he
built a new kitchen and patio
for our home?
    My Dad is special!
My Dad smells like grapefruit
cologne when he goes to weddings
and funerals. When I look at my
Dad when he comes home from
work as a, bus driver he
looks tired but always happy
to see his family. He loves
to eat noodles with soup. One
thing you don't know about
my Dad is that in August
he drives a truck to my Girl
Guide camp. Sometimes after
we eat dinner my Dad makes
funny faces like a monkey.
    My Dad is special!
June 20, 2010   Annette

Mary Cotrell and Jeanette Mumford, Grade 3 teachers at Sexsmith Elementary School, adapted this writing lesson for Father's Day. The published and illustrated writing pieces were given as gifts on Father's Day, no doubt bringing smiles and warm hearts to many dads.

This story strip is by a student in Grade 2.

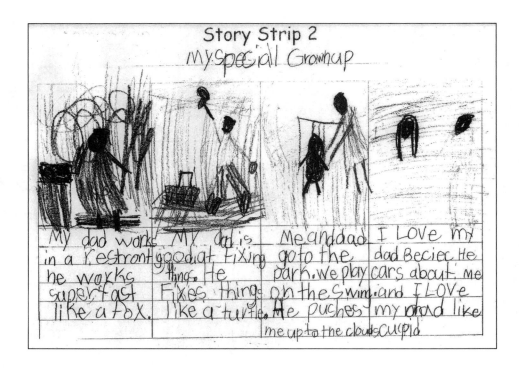

Story Strip 2
My Special Grownup

My dad works in a restront he works super fast like a fox.

My dad is good at fixing things. He fixes things like a turtle.

Me and dad go to the park. we play on the swing. He puches me up to the clouds

I Love my dad Beciec He cars about me and I LOVE my dad like cupid

Connecting to a Friend

Anchor Books for Connecting to a Friend

Aliki, *We Are Best Friends* (P)
Kathryn Cave, *That's What Friends Do* (P)
Sue Heap, *Red Rockets and Rainbow Jelly* (P)
Kevin Henkes, *Chester's Way* (P, I)
Rebecca C. Jones, *Matthew and Tilly* (I)

Sam McBratney, *I'm Sorry* (P)
Alexis O'Neil, *The Worst Best Friend* (P, I)
Mary Ann Rodman, *My Best Friend* (I)
Judith Viorst, *Rosie and Michael* (I)

Narrative Power: Climbing Story in Third Person

Technical Power: Adding Details (p. 43); Vocabulary (p. 48); Writing in the Third Person (p. 49)

Lesson 1: Planning

- Remind students that they are focusing their writing on inviting readers to make connections. Previous writing has included connecting to themselves, to feelings, and to special grown-ups. This week they will be focusing on connecting to something new.
- Share one or two of the suggested anchor books. Ask students to notice their own connections while you read. After reading, have them discuss and share a connection with a partner. Ask:

  What connections were you making? What did you notice about these books? (They were about friendships.)

  Explain that writing about a friend will help our readers to make connections to their own friends.

- Ask students to think about a special friend that they have and would like to write about.

  When did you become friends? What makes this friend special? What things do you like to do with this friend?

Invite students to go to their Memory Pockets to find a special memory they have of this friend.

Share the following with a partner:
- Name of your friend
- How you met
- Something you really like about your friend
- A special memory you shared with your friend

- Spend some time brainstorming triple-scoop words (see page 48) about friends.
- Pass out the Connecting to a Friend Planning Sheet (page 79) and have students work independently to complete the page.

Lesson 2: Writing

- Return students' Connecting to a Friend Planning Pages and have them share with a partner.
- Explain to students that they will be using the ideas from their planning sheets to write a piece about their friend. Explain that the writing pieces they have done until now had been walking stories but that today they are going to be writing a climbing story.

See page 37 in Chapter 3: Narrative Power for the lesson on walking and climbing story formats.

The idea for the writing came from your memory pocket but you are going to be writing it in third person.

- Model your example:

Teacher Model

Cheryl and Cassie were best friends. They wore the same clothes and loved the same singers and ate the same flavor of ice cream.

(Explain that this is the flat part of the story where you are setting the scene for the reader: introducing the characters and giving some details about them)

Cheryl and Cassie were in the same class at school. They were buddies when it was buddy reading and partners in P.E. They ate lunch together every day.

(Explain that these are a few more details)

One day, Cheryl made a joke about Cassie's new haircut and all the other kids laughed. Cassie's heart got tight and her eyes stung when she heard her friend making fun of her.

(Explain that this is where the story begins to climb up the hill because something happened)

The next day, Cheryl found Cassie sitting alone. "I'm sorry I made fun of your hair," she said. "I didn't mean to hurt your feelings." Cassie's heart loosened a little. "Thanks for saying sorry," she said.

(Explain that now you are starting to come back down the hill)

Cheryl and Cassie were friends again.

(Explain that now the story is finished and that your reader was not left stranded at the top of the hill!)

Emergent writers would most likely still be writing in first person, but are certainly capable of writing a climbing story with some guidance.

- Students can begin writing their own story about friendship, using their planning sheets to help them generate some details and examples.

Lessons 3 and 4

See page 61.

Story Strip for Emergent Writers: My Friend _____

My friend _____ is …	We like to…	One day…	Then…	Finally…

This story strip is by a student in Grade 2.

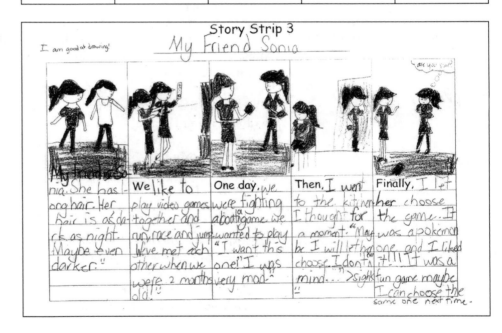

Connecting to a Sibling

See the Connecting to a Sibling Planning Sheet on page 80.

You might wish to do a lesson similar to Connecting to a Friend, but focusing on connecting to a sibling rather than a friend. Students can use a walking or climbing structure for this writing piece. For lessons, see pages 68–70.

Anchor Books for Connecting to a Sibling

Judy Bloom, *The Pain and the Great One* (I)
Anthony Browne, *My Brother* (P)
David MacPhail, *Sisters* (P)
Patricia Polacco, *My Rotten-Red-Headed-Older-Brother* (I)

Judith Viorst, *Super-Completely and Totally the Messiest* (P, I)
Charlotte Zolotow, *Big Sister and Little Sister* (P)

Connecting to a Bad Day

Anchor Books for Connecting to a Bad Day

Julia Cook, *The Worst Day of My Life, Ever!* (P)
Eugenie Fernandez, *The Difficult Day* (P)
Tom Lichtenheld, *What are You So Grumpy About?* (I)
Steve Metzger, *Dinofours: I'm Having a Bad Day!* (P)

Amy Krouse Rosenthal, *One of Those Days* (I)
Judith Viorst, *Alexander and the Terrible, Horrible, No Good, Very Bad Day* (P)

Narrative Power: Walking or Climbing Story (students can choose)

Technical Power: Writing in the Third Person (p. 49); Anchor Lines (p. 47); Adding Details (p. 43)

Lesson 1: Planning

- Remind students that you are working on writing that invites readers to make connections. Previous writing has included connecting to self, feelings, special grown-ups, friends. This week they will be focusing on connecting to something new.
- Share one or two of the suggested anchor books. Ask students to notice their own connections while you read. After reading, have students discuss and share a connection with a partner. Ask: What connections were you making? What did you notice about these books? (they are about bad days) Explain that almost everybody has bad days and that writing about your bad day will help readers make connections to a bad day they've had.
- Ask students to think about something that can turn a good day into a bad day. Record their ideas on the board or chart paper.

  Getting in trouble at home or school
  Losing something special
  A special plan gets cancelled or doesn't work out
  Losing an important game or not winning a prize

- Ask students to search their Memory Pockets for a bad day. Ask them to share the following with a partner:

  - When did it happen?
  - How did the day start?
  - What happened to turn it into a bad day?
  - How did you feel?

- Pass out the My Bad Day Planning Sheet (page 81) and invite students to record their ideas on it.

Lesson 2: Writing

This lesson can be adapted or repeated by focusing on Connecting to My Best Day Ever.
Anchor Book for Connecting to My Best Day Ever: Amy Krouse Rosenthal, *Yes Day!*

- Remind students that their writing focus this week is connecting to a bad day. Return their planning sheets and have students share them with a partner.
- Students can choose to write a climbing story about one particular bad day (like *A Difficult Day*) or a walking story describing a variety of bad day experiences (like *One of Those Days*). Remind them that, if they are writing a walking story, they will need to think about an anchor line (e.g., "… terrible, horrible, no-good, very bad day!"). Stories can be written in third person or first person.

Lessons 3 and 4

See page 61.

Story Strip for Emergent Writers: Connecting to a Bad Day

A bad day is when _____	Or when _____	Or when _____	But my worst day ever was when _____

Connecting to Memories

Anchor Books for Connecting to Memories

Jamie Lee Curtis, *When I was Little* (P)
Arthur Howard, *When I was Five* (P)
Sara O'Leary, *When You Were Small* (P, I)
Isabel Minhós Martins, *When I Was Born* (P)
Barbara Reid, *The Party* (P, I)

Cynthia Rylant, *Birthday Presents* (P, I)
Cynthia Rylant, *When I was Young in the Mountains* (P, I)
Charlotte Zolotow, *I Like to Be Little!* (P, I)

Narrative Power: Walking Story, First Person

Technical Power: Adding Details (p. 43); Anchor Lines (p. 47); Vocabulary (p. 48)

Lesson 1: Planning

- Remind students that you have been working on writing that invites readers to make connections. Previous writing has included connecting to feelings, special grown-ups, friends, and a bad day. This week they will be focusing on connecting to something new.
- Share one or two of the suggested anchor books. Ask students to notice their own connections while you read. After reading, have students discuss and share a connection with a partner. Ask: What connections were you making? What did you notice about these books? (they are about memories of being little)

  All of us have special memories of when we were little, of funny things we said and did, things we weren't allowed to do, things we learned. Writing about your own personal memories of when you were little can help your reader make connections to when they were young.

- Invite students to bring some of their own photographs to school and encourage them to ask their parents about any stories or memories they might be able to share with them about their early years. Brainstorm some possible ideas to write about:

  - Learning to walk
  - My first words
  - My favorite blanket or stuffed toy
  - My first foods or early eating habits
  - Funny things I said
  - Funny things I did
  - My first birthday party

- Places I liked to go
- Games I liked to play
- Early activities: swimming, singing time, etc.

- Ask students to search their Memory Pockets for their memories of when they were little. Ask them to turn to a partner and finish this sentence: "When I was little, I…"
- Pass out the Connecting to When I Was Little Planning Sheet (page 82) and invite students to record their ideas on them. This could be something that they take home to complete so that their parents can help them.

Lesson 2: Writing

- Remind students that their writing focus this week is connecting to memories. Return their planning sheets and have students share them with a partner.
- Reread *When I Was Four* by Jamie Lee Curtis. Ask students what they liked and what they noticed about the book. (It is personal; anchor line "When I was little"; it is in the first person)
- Remind students that they will be writing a walking story in the first person. Go over some of the writing techniques they can use in their piece: Anchor Lines, Adding Details. As a review of adding details, write these two examples on the board and discuss the difference.

  When I was little, I cried a lot.
  (This is something that happens to everyone)
  When I was little, I got the hiccups every time I ate eggs.
  (This is something that adds a detail and makes your writing unique)

Lessons 3 and 4

See page 61. During Lesson 4: Publishing and Sharing, students might choose to include an illustration or a photograph of themselves when they were little.

Story Strip for Emergent Writers: Connecting to When I Was Little

When I was little, I used to call _____ (or say)…	When I was little, I had… (a special toy or blanket)	When I was little, I liked to … (something you did or somewhere you liked to go)	When I was little, I… _____ But now I…

This story strip is by a student in Grade 2.

Connecting to Me Planning Sheet

Name: _____

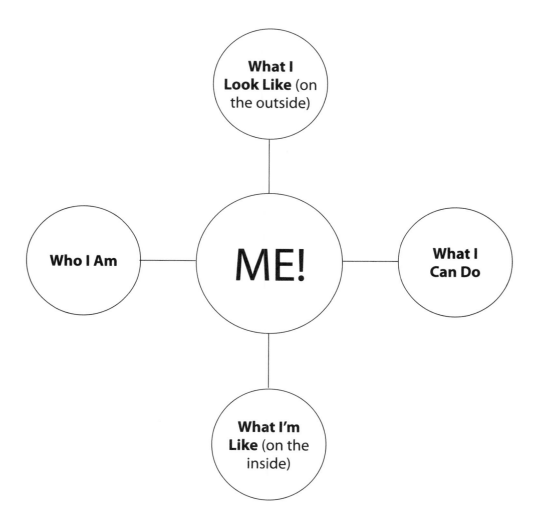

Connecting to Feelings Planning Sheet

Name: _____

Search your Memory Pocket to find examples of these different feelings. Try to give examples that are unique to your experiences.

I felt/feel **mad** when… _____

I felt/feel **embarrassed** when … _____

I felt/feel **jealous** when … _____

I felt/feel **nervous** when… _____

I felt/feel **surprised** when … _____

I felt/feel **bored** when… _____

I felt/feel **sad** when… _____

I felt/feel **scared** when… _____

I felt/feel **proud** when… _____

I felt/feel **disappointed** when… _____

I felt/feel **excited** when… _____

I felt/feel **frustrated** when… _____

Now choose one of your emotions that you would like to expand in a writing piece. Try to choose an experience that is unique to you.

_____

Pembroke Publishers ©2011 *Writing Power* by Adrienne Gear ISBN 978-1-55138-263-0

Connecting to a Special Grown-Up Planning Sheet

Name: _____

My _____'s name is _____

My _____ was born in _____ (country)

Hair: _____ Eyes: _____

Hobbies: _____

Job: _____

Good at: _____

Something I like to do with _____ :

_____

_____

Something interesting that you might not know about my _____:

_____

_____

It makes me laugh when my _____

_____

_____

My _____ always says (favorite saying or expression)

" _____ "

Pembroke Publishers ©2011 *Writing Power* by Adrienne Gear ISBN 978-1-55138-263-0

Connecting to a Special Grown-Up Planning Sheet cont'd

It makes me feel special and loved when my _____

_____

_____

A special/favorite memory of my _____ is of when

_____

_____

_____

*3 **Triple-Scoop** words to describe my _____:*

_____   _____   _____

6 Senses of my _____:

See:	Smell:
Hear:	Taste:
Feel (touch):	Feel (heart):

Pembroke Publishers ©2011 *Writing Power* by Adrienne Gear ISBN 978-1-55138-263-0

Connecting to a Friend Planning Sheet

Name: _____

My friend's name: _____

We met _____ (when and where)

Things I like to do with my friend:

_____

_____

Four triple-scoop words I would use to describe my friend:

_____ _____

_____ _____

My friend is special to me because

_____

_____

A special memory I have with my friend was the time when we

_____

_____

A problem I once had with my friend:

_____

_____

This is how we solved the problem:

_____

_____

Pembroke Publishers ©2011 *Writing Power* by Adrienne Gear ISBN 978-1-55138-263-0

Connecting to a Sibling

My brother/sister's name: _____   He/She is _____ old.

Four triple-scoop words I would use to describe my sister/brother:

_____   _____

_____   _____

Something I really admire/respect about my sister/brother is

_____

Something I don't really like about my brother/sister:

_____

Every day my brother/sister _____

I get annoyed at my brother/sister when he/she

_____

_____

One thing you might not know about my brother/sister is that

_____

_____

A special memory I have with my brother/sister is of when

_____

_____

Pembroke Publishers ©2011 *Writing Power* by Adrienne Gear ISBN 978-1-55138-263-0

My Bad Day Planning Sheet

Name: _____

When it happened: _____

Where it happened: _____

The day started… (describe how the day started out before it turned into a bad day)

_____

_____

What happened? (describe what happened to make it a bad day)

_____

_____

The worst part about the day was (describe what you remember most about the bad day)

_____

_____

End of the day (describe how your bad day ended):

_____

_____

What triple-scoop words would you use to describe this bad day?

_____   _____   _____

You will be writing this story in **third person**. Use your experience but change the "me" to a character.

My character's name is: _____

Connecting to When I Was Little Planning Sheet

Name: _____

A favorite toy or game *When I was little, I used to…*	A funny word I said *When I was little, I…*	Something I liked to to *When I was little, I used to…*
_____ _____ _____ _____ _____ _____	_____ _____ _____ _____ _____ _____	_____ _____ _____ _____ _____ _____

Something I used to think
When I was little, I used to think…

_____
_____
_____
_____
_____
_____

But now I think…

_____
_____
_____
_____
_____
_____

Something I wasn't allowed to do
When I was little, I…

_____
_____
_____
_____
_____

But now I…

_____
_____
_____
_____
_____

Pembroke Publishers ©2011 *Writing Power* by Adrienne Gear ISBN 978-1-55138-263-0

8 Inviting Readers to Visualize

After a long car trip listening to a book on tape of *The Hatchet*, a young boy reports to his mother, "That was the best movie I've ever seen." Visualizing is a strategy used by readers to help them see in their minds what is unfolding within the pages of the text. Visualizing is more likely to occur when there are no visuals accompanying the text, and it occurs more specifically during the process of reading rather than afterward.

There are certain texts that invite us to visualize more easily, more readily, and more frequently. Why do some books invite visual images, while others don't? We have to look to the writing. Authors, like artists, create visual images. The only difference is that we see the artist's vision with our eyes; we see the author's vision with our brains. An artist chooses and uses various paints from his/her palette, mixing and arranging them carefully on the canvas to create an image for us to see with our eyes. An author chooses and uses words, mixing and arranging them on the page to create an image for us to see in our minds.

Exceptional word choice breeds vivid images. As writers, becoming more aware of this can only enhance our ability and our desire to choose and use our words more effectively. Many teachers recognize word choice as one of the traits of good writing we teach our students. Through the writing traits approach, students learn that word choice is one of the important aspects of good writing— but do they actually know why? Writing Power takes this one step forward by introducing writers to purpose. With this alocognitive approach, we are teaching students a deeper awareness. Why is it important to choose and use words effectively in our writing? Answer: Because we know good readers visualize and we want to support them in this process. We can do this by becoming a word artist and painting pictures with our words.

Thinking Power to Visualize

Most often, readers create mental images by retrieving pictures that are already stored in their Memory Pockets. In other words, they make a connection with something they have seen or know about and that is what helps them to create the image. It is more challenging to visualize things we have not personally experienced. This all happens in an instant, but if we were to slow it down, we might see it as similar to searching through archives of photo files to find a specific photo. Our brains search through our files until we find an image we can use to support the text we are reading. When a reader has no specific experience or memory from which to draw, the Imagination Pocket can often support visualizing. Readers who were first introduced to Hogwarts School of Witchcraft and Wizardy, for example, had never personally experienced it; however, J.K. Rowling's rich descriptions helped us all to "see" it with our imaginations.

Lesson: Introducing Writing that Invites Visualization

- Write the word *visualize* on the board. Ask students what it means and what it has to do with reading (making a picture in your mind; good readers visualize while they read to help them understand the story better).
- Try some quick visualizing exercises. Have students close their eyes and visualize a word; e.g., *butterfly, puppy, delicious, slowly.* Invite students to share what they visualized with a partner. Ask students several questions about their mental pictures: e.g., *Was it a monarch? Was it in flight? Was it on a flower? Did you see a background?* Discuss the fact that people visualize differently because we have different pictures stored in our brains. Ask students: Where do our pictures come from? (Memory Pocket) Ask students where they might go to find a picture of a castle if they have no memory or experience of one (Imagination Pocket or Fact Pocket).
- Visualizing Activity: Read through a picture book, but do not show the students the pictures; cover up the book jacket, if you can. Ask students to visualize while you read. Pass out blank paper. Read the story a second time and have the students draw/sketch images while they are listening to the story. Invite them to record two or three picture words. Have students share and compare their pictures with a partner.
- After the activity, discuss the process with your class:

How were you able to "see" these images, even though I didn't show you the pictures?

Sometimes I read a book and I'm able to really "see" it, and other times I can't. Why is this? Why are some books more visual than others?

An author is like an artist. An artist begins with a blank canvas and creates an image by mixing paints and arranging them on the canvas. A writer begins with a blank page but, instead of paint, what does an author use to "paint the picture"? (words) As writers, we need to learn to paint pictures with our words because we want our readers to visualize.

Explain to students that many writing techniques they will be learning will help them paint pictures for their readers to visualize.

- End-of-lesson reflection:

Today we spent some time talking about visualizing. Good readers visualize while they read. But we now know that they are able to do this because the writer used words to paint the picture for the reader. In the next few weeks, we will be learning how to paint pictures with our words to help our readers visualize.

Visualizing an Apple

Lesson 1: Planning

- Remind your students that good readers visualize when they read. Ask them how writers help their readers visualize (by choosing words that can help "paint a picture" in the reader's mind).
- Pass out writing samples (see page 102) and ask students to read through both samples. (Primary teachers can read samples to the class aloud). Have students discuss with a partner (or with the class) the following:

Instead of anchor books, use the writing samples found on page 102 as anchor texts.

Narrative Power: Walking Story

Technical Power: Six Senses (p. 47); Similes (p. 45); Vocabulary (p. 48)

What did you notice about the two samples? How were they the same? How were they different? (Sample 1 tells information about an apple; Sample 2 describes what an apple looks like, feels like, tastes like, smells like, etc.)

Which sample helped you to visualize? Why could we visualize better with one sample than the other? What did the writer of Sample 2 do to help us visualize?

Invite students to underline words or phrases that were particularly visual.

- Explain that writers can help their readers visualize by focusing on the reader's senses:

Good writers certainly include words to help readers see things by describing what they look like. *Vision* means "to see" and sometimes we think visualizing is just about what we see inside our heads. But visualizing is more than just creating pictures that we see. It also is about using all of our other senses.

Brainstorm the six senses: sight, sound, taste, smell, feel outside (touch), feel inside (emotion).

As writers, we don't want our readers to just see what we are writing about; we want them to be able to smell and taste and feel it too.

Word trading is a great way for students to give and receive ideas from a partner. If students see a word they like on a partner's list, they can add it to their own list. However, in exchange they must now give one of their words to their partner.

- Pass out the Visualizing an Apple Planning Sheet (page 102) and invite students to begin brainstorming "senses" words about an apple. Encourage four or five words per sense. After students have generated several words independently, invite them to share their words with a partner and do some word trading.

Lesson 2: Writing

- Using their planning sheet, the students develop a piece of writing about an apple that will create a strong visual for the reader. They are to use in their writing as many senses words from their planning sheet as possible. Remind students to try not to simply tell their readers about an apple, but to really try to paint a picture of an apple using words. Encourage students to use colorful triple-scoop words and similes in their writing. You might model a few words to get students on the right track: e.g., Taste words: *sweet, sour, juicy, grainy, delicious, crunchy.*

Lesson 3: Conferencing and Editing for all Invitations to Visualize

When students conference with a partner, suggest that they listen to their partner with their eyes closed. Encourage them to make comments on how the partner's writing helped them to visualize. When editing, remind students they can use either the 3, 2, 1…Edit! or 1, 2, 3, 4—Edit! (page 20) checklist to make at least four changes to improve their writing. Teachers can conference with two or three students each week. (See Writing Power Conference Record on page 23.)

Lesson 4: Publishing and Sharing for all Invitations to Visualize

Students might wish to draw an illustration to accompany their writing when developing a published copy. Choose two or three students to read their pieces aloud to the class.

Story Strip for Emergent Writers: The Apple

Michelle Sprintzios, Grade 5 teacher at Sexsmith Elementary School, accompanied this writing lesson with an art lesson on still life art, bringing real apples into the classroom and inviting students to practice careful and accurate apple drawings to accompany their writing.

Encourage primary students to use similes when they are writing. They can use the planning sheet on page 102, but expect that they will only record two or three words per sense.

PICTURE (describe apple's shape and color)	PICTURE (describe what an apple feels like)	PICTURE (describe apple's smell)	PICTURE (describe apple's taste and sound)

Visualizing the Seasons

Anchor Books for Visualizing the Seasons

All the Seasons
John Burningham, *Seasons* (P)
Myra Cohn Livingston, *Calendar* (P, I)
Bill Martin Jr., *The Turning of the Year* (P, I)
Il Sung Na, *Snow Rabbit, Spring Rabbit: A Book of Changing Seasons* (P)
Lynn Plourde, *Wild Child* (I)
Eileen Spinelli, *Here Comes the Year!* (P, I)

Fall
Lois Ehlert, *Red Leaf, Yellow Leaf* (P)
Douglas Florian, *Autumnblings* (P, I)
Linda Glassner, *It's Fall – Celebrate the Seasons!* (P)
Sebastian Meschenmoser, *Waiting for Winter* (P, I)
Kelly Nidey, *When Autumn Falls* (P, I)
Heather Patterson, *Thanks for Thanksgiving* (P, I)
Julia Rawlinson, *Fletcher and the Falling Leaves* (P)
Cynthia Rylant, *In November* (I)
Eileen Spinelli, *I Know It's Autumn* (P, I)

Winter
Jean Craighead George, *Dear Rebecca, Winter is Here* (I)

Denise Flemming, *The First Day of Winter* (P)
Douglas Florian, *Winter Eyes* (P, I)
Il Sung Na, *Brrr—A Book of Winter* (P)
Lynn Plourde, *Winter Waits* (I)
Barbara Seuling, *Winter Lullaby* (P)
Lauren Stringer, *Winter Is the Warmest Season* (P, I)
Cynthia Rylant, *Long Night Moon* (I)
Nancy Van Laan, *When Winter Comes* (P, I)

Spring
Jan Carr, *Splish, Splash, Spring* (P)
Douglas Florian, *Handsprings* (P, I)
Linda Glassner, *It's Spring* (P)
Lynn Plourde, *Spring's Sprung* (I)
Bob Raczka, *Spring Things* (P, I)

Summer
Nina Crew, *One Hot Summer Day* (P, I)
Douglas Florian, *Summersaults* (P, I)
Linda Glassner, *It's Summer* (P)
Nikki McClure, *Mama, Is it Summer Yet?* (P)
Lynn Plourde, *Summer's Vacation* (I)

Lesson 1: Planning

Narrative Power: Walking Story

Technical Power: Similes (p. 45); Six Senses and Anchor Lines (p. 47); Vocabulary (p. 48)

- Remind students that good readers visualize when they read and good writers help them do that by painting pictures with their words.
- If you are able to gather a few of the suggested anchor books, you can group the books into seasons. Divide the class into five groups: each of four groups will get anchor books on one of the four seasons; the final group will get anchor books on all the seasons. Invite students to take a few minutes to read and look through the books in their groups and to notice what their group of books has in common. Invite students to find a phrase or sentence from one of the books that really helped them paint a picture in their minds.

- Each group reports back to the class what they noticed that their books had in common. Students can read aloud their favorite visualizing phrase. You might choose to record some of these phrases on a chart entitled *Writing Inviting VISUALIZING*.
- Pass out Visualizing Seasons Planning Sheet, two-sided copies of page 102 and 104. On the front of the planning page are the four seasons. Tell students you are going to give them only two minutes to work on each season box. Encourage them to include colors, sounds, smells, activities, weather—anything they can think of. After completing two boxes, students can do some word trading (see margin note on page 85) with a partner for one minute. Once the four boxes are complete, students need to look over their sheets and determine which season they will choose as the subject for their longer writing piece. They can record this at the bottom of the front page and then complete the back of their planning sheet, focusing on the season they selected.

This sample is by a student in Grade 5.

Lesson 2: Writing

- Return the Visualizing Seasons Planning Sheets and have students share their season words with a partner. Explain that the topic of their writing is a season, but their goal as writers is to help readers visualize the season—to put themselves into the text and feel as though they are right there, smelling, tasting, and seeing the season, instead of just reading about a season. This piece will be a walking story in the first person. Remind students that they need to organize their writing and group their ideas around their senses, so that each section focuses on one. They can use an anchor line to keep the piece steady.
- Model your writing:

Teacher Model

Winter

In winter, I see snow shining like fairy dust. Lopsided snowmen with crooked pebble smiles stand on guard in yards and parks. Footprints lead in different directions, criss-crossing paths across the flat whiteness. Grey clouds hang heavy with more snow and I watch my white breath disappear like a ghost in the cold air. I see winter.

I hear winter, shouting with laughter down slippery slopes and across frozen ponds…

Lessons 3 and 4

See page 88.

Story Strip for Emergent Writers: Visualizing a Season

Primary students can choose one season for their topic. Remind them to write a sentence and then add a detail. You can model one example:

Teacher Model

In winter I see brown tree trunks with white arms. I see snowmen guarding the park. I see winter.

In _____ I see…	In _____ I hear…	In _____ I taste…	In _____ I feel…

Visualizing Weather

Anchor Books for Visualizing Weather

Snow
Marion Dane Bauer, *Snow* (P)
Nancy White Carlstrom, *The Snow Speaks* (P, I)
Ezra Jack Keats, *The Snowy Day* (P)
Wong Herbert Lee, *Tracks in the Snow* (P)
Lynn Plourde, *Snow Day* (P)
Cynthia Rylant, *Snow* (I)
Komako Sakai, *Snow Day* (P)
Alvin Tresselt, *White Snow, Bright Snow* (P, I)
Werner Zimmerman, *Snow Day* (I)

Wind
Frank Asch, *Like a Windy Day* (P)
Halina Below, *The Windy Day* (P, I)
Marie Hall Ets, *Gilberto and the Wind* (P, I)
Anna Milbourne, *The Windy Day* (P, I)

Rain
Marion Dane Bauer, *Rain* (P)
Karen Hesse, *Come On Rain* (P, I)
Robert Kalan, *Rain* (P, I)

Wong Herbert Lee, *Who Likes Rain?* (P)
Jonathan London, *Puddles* (P, I)
Bill Martin Jr., *Listen to the Rain* (P, I)
Anna Milbourne, *The Rainy Day* (P)
Mary Lyn Ray, *Red Rubber Boot Day* (P, I)
Alvin Tresselt, *Rain, Drop, Splash* (P)

Sun
Donald Crews, *Cloudy Day – Sunny Day* (P)
Alice Low, *Summer* (P)
Anna Milbourne, *The Sunny Day* (P, I)
Cynthia Rider, *Sunny Day* (P)
Eileen Spinelli, *Heat Wave* (P, I)

Narrative Power: Walking Story

Technical Power: Personification (p. 50); Vocabulary (p. 48); Six Senses (p. 47)

Lesson 1: Planning

- Remind students that good writers want to invite their readers to visualize. Ask students how writers are able to do this.
- Pass anchor books to groups of students. Give them time to look through the books and try to find examples of writing that helps them visualize. Ask them what the books have in common (they are all about different kinds of weather). Explain that the writing focus for the week will be writing about weather.
- Pass out the Visualizing Weather Planning Sheet (page 105). Students can complete the top portion of the planning sheet by brainstorming words that they associate with each type of weather. Remind them to include such things as color, texture, feelings, and senses. You might give them a time limit for brainstorming (one minute per box) and then invite them to share their boxes with a partner. After completing the top portion, students choose one specific type of weather that will be the focus for their writing. They can then complete the bottom portion of the planning sheet by brainstorming senses words describing that weather type.

Lesson 2: Writing

- Return the Visualizing Weather Planning Sheets and give students time to share their plans with a partner. If students wish, they can find a partner who has selected the same weather type and do some word trading with them.
- Remind students that good writers try to help their readers visualize. Explain that they will be using the writer's technique of personification to do this.
- Remind students that personification is when a writer gives human characteristics to something that is not human.

Today we will be turning our weather into a person and writing in first person as that weather. That means you will be writing as the weather, using "I." The piece will be a walking story and we can use the six senses and an anchor line to organize our ideas (as we did for our piece on a season).

You might give students the Personification Match sheet (page 56) to use on their selected weather prior to writing.

- Encourage students to group their ideas together: for example, what the weather looks like; what it does (actions); what it sounds and feels like; what it tastes and smells like; what people say, think, or feel about it. The anchor line could be as simple as "I am _____"
- Model your writing:

Teacher Model

I am the snow, cold and white, that falls silently on your grass. I cover the green and spread my white blanket over the streets and the sidewalks. I bring delight to many, headaches to some, and joy to all school kids when I turn a school day into a snow day. I am the snow.

RAIN

I am the rain. I fall from grey clouds and turn the sidewalks black. I help flowers grow in spring and I wash snow away in winter. I sometimes fall when you are trying to have a piknic and ruin all your fun. I can make rainbows appear in the sky with a little help from my friend sun. I make drumming sounds and pitter-patter splish-splash sounds and I go tap tap on the car window. Sometimes when you our tring to sleep is when I make the drip drip drip sounds. (He! He!) I bring water to drink for pepol with no taps. You may like me or maybe not but I'm here to stay. I am RAIN!

Lessons 3 and 4

See pages 85–86.

Story Strip for Emergent Writers

Primary teachers can adapt this writing lesson for their students; however, even younger children are capable of trying new writing techniques and would be able to incorporate personification into their writing.

I am _____. I _____ (Describe what this weather looks like—color, shape, etc.)	I am _____. I _____ (Describe what this weather does and how it does it)	I am _____. I _____ (Describe what this weather sounds like and tastes like)	I am _____ I _____ (Describe how this weather feels)

Visualizing a Special Place

Anchor Books for Visualizing a Special Place

Margaret Wise Brown, *Big Red Barn* (P)
Laurel Croza, *I Know Here* (I)
Ralph Fletcher, *When Twilight Comes Twice* (I)
Nancy Hundal, *Camping* (I)
Nancy Hundal, *Prairie Summer* (I)
Norton Jester, *Hello, Goodbye Window* (P, I)
Patricia MacLaughlan, *All the Places to Love* (P, I)
Jesse S. Ostrow, *My Garden* (P)
Gary Paulson, *Canoe Days* (I)
Dave Pilchy, *The Paper Boy* (P, I)
Pam Munroz Ryan, *Hello Ocean* (I)

Margaret Ruirs, *When We Go Camping* (P, I)
Cynthia Rylant, *Night in the Country* (P, I)
Cynthia Rylant, *When I Was Young in the Mountains* (P, I)
Paul Showers, *The Listening Walk* (P)
Rosemary Wells, *Night Sounds, Morning Colors* (P)
E.B. White, *Charlotte's Web* (description of the barn) (I)
Kari-Lynn Winters, *On my Walk* (P)
Audrey Wood, *There's The Sea* (P)
Charlotte Zolotow, *The Seashore Book* (I)

Narrative Power: Walking Story

Technical Power: Anchor Lines (p. 47); Six Senses (p. 47); Similes (p. 45); Voice (p. 48)

Lesson 1: Planning

- Remind students that you are focusing on writing that invites readers to visualize.

  Writers need to think about choosing and using words that can help their readers paint a picture in their mind.

- Share the titles of one or two anchor books and ask students if they know what these books have in common (they are all about places, or special places). Read one of the anchor books, but don't show the pictures. Invite students to try to visualize while you read and to listen especially for any words or phrases that help them visualize. After reading, invite students to share their strongest visual image with a partner. Ask: What did you see? What picture words do you notice?
- Explain that these books focus on special places, places that are meaningful to the author. Note that they describe these special places in detail and, when we read them, it helps us to visualize.
- Invite students to go to their Memory Pockets to find a special place they have stored there.

  Here are some ideas: your house, your bedroom, your bed, a favorite spot in your backyard, your grandparent's house, your aunt's house, a summer vacation place, your favorite campsite, a hockey rink, a park you know very well. The place you choose needs to be a place where you've spent a lot of time and that you know very well.

  Discourage students from choosing big places, such as Disneyland or a mall. Encourage them to choose a place that is very personal and that only they would know what is like. Have students share their special place with a partner, explaining why it is special to them.

- Visualizing exercise:

  I'd like everyone to close your eyes and visualize your special place. If it is a house, I want you to go to that house; if it is a park, put yourself in that park; if it is your neighborhood, begin walking down the street. Look around you. What do you see? What sounds do you hear? Can you smell anything? Taste anything? What feelings do you get when you're there? Who do you think about when you think about being in this special place?

- Have students share their special place with a partner: something they saw, heard, tasted, smelled, felt in their special place.
- Pass out the Visualizing My Special Place Planning Sheet (page 106). Remind students to include ideas from the visualizing exercise while they complete it.

This planning sample is by a student in Grade 5.

Lesson 2: Writing

- Remind students about the special places they visualized the day before and explain that today they will be using their planning sheet to write a piece.
- Discuss anchor lines used by other authors in the books you read:

  "I know here…"
  "When I was young in the mountains…"
  "Where else could you….?"

- Model your own writing, using an anchor line and ideas from your planning sheet. Ask the students to listen for the anchor line and senses.

Teacher Model

My Special Place
I know home. Home is where I live—my house, my place of belonging. I know the wide front steps that lead to our porch. I know the view of the mountains I can see from the porch—blue in the summer, gray with white sprinkles in the winter. I know the mixed-up pile of shoes in the entrance way…shoes looking for partners and feet to fill them. I know the sound of Bailey's paws as she clicks on the hardwood floor and wiggles her furry bottom over to greet me. I have seen her furry-wiggle-bottom-greeting hundreds of times but it still makes me smile. I know other sounds of this home—the laughing, the snoring, the happy shouting (and the sometimes mad shouting), the music, the TV, the clatter, and the quiet. I know this kitchen—the bulletin board crammed with school notices, pictures, allowance charts, art, homework bins, baseball and hockey schedules, and a color-coded calendar that sometimes makes my head spin. I know the smells of this home—cinnamon buns, chocolate chip cookies, the fireplace, wet fur, and stinky hockey gear. I know this home, the home I live in, the home I love.

- Students can begin writing their piece, focusing on choosing words to help their readers visualize their special place. Encourage students to write as if they are actually *in* their special place and they are describing it to someone who can't see it. Remind them to try to organize their sentences so that they are not just listing: e.g., I see this…; I see that…; I see…

Lessons 3 and 4

See pages 85–86.

Story Strip for Emergent Writers: My Special Place

My special place is… (tell where it is, what it is, why is it special)	In my special place, I can see…	In my special place, I can hear (or smell)…	In my special place, I feel…

I know here

I know here. Here is where I see new born Baby birds. I see the Butterflys gracefully flutter by, Kids riding thier bike across the street. In my Special Place I can hear my both neighbor's dc barking and waging it's tail with joy. I can hear seagulls and a Hawk screamin at each other. I call out "stop it, it's too loud". I hear the mail man closing the mail box. I can hear children screaming in my special place. In my Special place I can smell the flowers filling the backyard, I can smell the neigbor's barbecueing hamburge and hot dogs. In my special place I can feel the wind run against my elbow and the tall smooth grass against my leg. My cousins come and we play game in my special place. While we play my neighbor stops and say " good afternoon, how are you doing? In my special place

Visualizing an Imaginary Place

Anchor Books for Visualizing an Imaginary Place

Kevin Henkes, *My Garden* (P)
Anne Mazer, *Salamander Room* (P, I)
James Mayhew, *Starlight Sailor* (P)

Eric Rohmann, *The Cinder-Eyed Cats* (P, I)
Sarah L. Thomson, *Imagine a Place* (I)
Douglas Wood, *A Quiet Place* (I)

Narrative Power: Walking Story

Technical Power: Anchor Lines
(p. 47); Similes (p. 45); Adding Details
(p. 43); Vocabulary (p. 48)

Lesson 1: Planning

- Remind students that writers help their readers visualize by painting pictures with their words. Ask students where writers get their ideas for writing. Review the concept of Brain Pockets (see page 33 for lesson on Brain Pockets). Explain that writers find ideas from different pockets when they are writing different things:

  If we are writing information, we will be using facts stored in our Fact Pockets. When we write a story about friendship or feelings, we might find ideas stored in our Memory Pockets. Today you will be finding ideas for your writing in your Imagination Pocket.

- Share one or two of the anchor books. Ask students to listen for similes. Ask them to listen for anchor lines; e.g., "Imagine a place where…" "In my garden …."
- Explain that this week's writing will focus on an imaginary place. This could be an imaginary garden, forest, pond, park, jungle, or meadow. Remind students that when writers write descriptions of a place, they need to add as many details as they can so that the reader feels as if they are actually there, in that place. They also need to organize their writing by grouping their ideas together; otherwise, their readers might get confused.
- Brainstorm three or four "idea boxes" to organize notes for describing an imaginary place:

  - What it looks like (colors, animals, plants)
  - What tastes and smells you would you find there
  - What interesting or unusual things might happen there
  - Something that happened once when you were there

- Visualizing exercise: Have students close their eyes and visualize their imaginary place.

  What do you see? Smell? Hear? Take a walk through your special place and notice everything around you. Look up. Look down. What interesting or unusual things can you see?

  Remind students that this is no ordinary place, but a place that is completely imaginary.

- Pass out the Visualizing an Imaginary Place Planning Sheet (see page 105). Students can spend time recording ideas on the sheet. Explain that they do not need to write complete sentences, but just jot down ideas.

Lesson 2: Writing

- Return the Visualizing a Place Planning Sheets and invite students to tell a partner all about their imaginary place. Remind students of the writing techniques that they will be focusing on, which include Similes, Adding Details, Anchor Lines, Vocabulary. Also encourage them to use their four "idea boxes" to help them organize their writing. Remind them not to write a list, but to write a fact and then add a detail.

- Model your writing:

Teacher Model

My Garden

In my garden, the sun shines every day, even when it's raining everywhere else! There are flowers that grow as tall as trees and strawberries that grow as big as a beach ball. In my garden, there is a tree that grows every kind of fruit. All you need to do is say the name of a fruit and it will grow. In my garden, if I plant alphabet letters, books will grow. Once, I picked a book and lay in a giant tulip and read to the birds. The sparrows liked the quiet books and the crows liked joke books. In my garden, the worms play checkers with the caterpillars. The worms usually win! In my garden, butterflies fly near my ear and whisper secrets. When it rains in my garden, the rain tastes like lemonade. Snow tastes like marshmallows and rainbows come in all different flavors!

Lessons 3 and 4

See pages 85–86.

Story Strip for Emergent Writers: In My Imaginary Garden

In my garden, I see…	In my garden… (something usual that you might see in your garden)	In my garden, if I plant a _____, a _____ grows.	Once, in my garden…

This story strip is by a student in Grade 2.

Visualizing Color

Anchor Books for Visualizing Color

Menena Cottin, *The Black Book of Colors* (P, I)
Jimmy Liao, *Sounds of Color* (I)
Mary O'Neill, *Hailstones and Halibut Bones* (P, I)
Dr. Seuss, *My Many Colored Days* (P)

Joyce Sidman, *Red Sings From the Treetops: A Year in Colors* (I)
Audrey Wood, *There's the Sea: A Book of Colors* (P, I)

Narrative Power: Poetry

Technical Power: Six Senses (p. 47), Vocabulary (p. 48)

Lesson 1: Planning

- Remind students that they are working on writing that helps their readers visualize. Ask them how writers can help their readers to visualize. Read from one or two of the anchor books and invite students to visualize when you are reading. Discuss some of the images that they were able to create in their minds. Ask the students what the books had in common (all about colors).
- Explain that this week, they will be writing about colors. Pass out the Visualizing Color Planning Sheet 1 (page 108) and explain that students will be working on two planning sheets. The first one is for brainstorming everything that they can think of that is that color. This can be done with a partner and can be timed:

  Write down everything you can think of that is red in one minute. Go!

  Explain that students should not include things that come in more than one color: e.g., crayon might be red, but crayons come in all colors, so it should not be included.

- Once the students have finished brainstorming, they will need to choose one color that will be the topic of their writing piece. Pass out the Visualizing Color Planning Sheet 2 (page 109).
- Model for students how they should brainstorm senses words that are connected to that color.

Teacher Model

RED

Sight	Smell	Sound
Strawberry	Strawberry sweet	Love
Heart	Sweet apple	danger –
Blood	Cherry sweet	blood
Rose	Fire - danger	fire truck loud
Raspberry	Rose fresh	crackling fire
Fire truck	Red pepper sweet	plucking
Tomato		strawberries
Canada flag		
Taste	**Touch**	**Feeling**
Sweet strawberry	hot fire	Love
Sour cranberry	cut pain	Stop
Bitter radish	soft love	Danger
Crunchy juicy apple	thorn prickly rose	
Red liquorice chewy		

Lesson 2: Writing

- Return the Visualizing Color Planning Sheets. Students can share and compare their ideas with a partner.
- Explain that students will be using the ideas from their planning pages to help them write. They will be writing a poem about a color that will include all of the senses. The poem will follow a pattern of opposites.
- Model your writing:

Teacher Model

Red
Red tastes sweet like a juicy strawberry, but can be tangy like a ripe tomato.
Red can be quiet like the Canadian flag waving in the breeze or as loud as a fire truck screeching down the street.
Red is smooth like the skin of an apple, or sharp and prickly like a thorn on a rose.
Red is kindness and love or anger and danger.

Discuss how each line is focuses on a sense, but pairs up examples as opposites.

- Students begin to write, using ideas from their planning page. Remind them that poetry looks different from prose because you don't continue writing to the end of the line.

This sample is by a student in Grade 4.

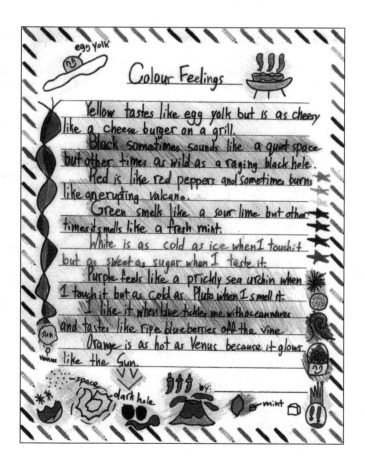

Lessons 3 and 4

See pages 85–86.

Visualizing a Character

Anchor Books for Visualizing a Character

Roald Dahl, *Charlie and the Chocolate Factory*, description of Willy Wonka (late P, I)

Roald Dahl, *BFG*, description of BFG (late P, I)

Roald Dahl, *James and the Giant Peach*, description of Aunt Spike and Aunt Sponge (late P, I)

Roald Dahl, *The Witches*, description of the witch (late P, I)

J.K. Rowling, *Harry Potter and the Philosopher's Stone*, description of Dumbledore (late P, I)

There is no better author for descriptions of characters that invite readers to visualize than Roald Dahl. He models how to bring a reader into the text and let them "see" the characters so clearly that readers feel as if they are standing directly in front of them.

Narrative Power: Standing Story

Technical Power: Similes (p. 45); Adding Details (p. 43); Vocabulary (p. 48); First Impressions (p. 51)

Depending on the grade you teach, you might want to project these descriptions on an overhead or interactive whiteboard while you read, so that students can see as well as hear the words as you read them.

Lesson 1: Planning

- Remind students that the focus for their writing is to help their readers to visualize. Read aloud one or two of the character descriptions from the anchor books and invite students to visualize while you read. Have students share and compare what they visualized in partners.

- Discuss what the writing was about (describing a character) and why the writing made it so easy for readers to visualize. Tell students that good writers want to make sure that their readers can see the characters the authors are writing about.

This week's writing will be focusing on helping our readers to visualize a character.

- Brainstorm or create a class web for what might need to be included in a description of a character if we really wanted to help readers to visualize the character. Ideas might include height, body shape, hair style and color, eyes, nose, mouth, clothes or style, voice, interesting or unique features (scars, tattoos, etc.).

- Explain that when a writer is trying to create a character, there are four main things that they need to consider:

  Physical Traits or what your character looks like: size, shape, skin, eyes, hair
  Personality Traits or how your character acts: clever, smart, nervous, angry
  Kinesthetic Traits or how your character moves: waddles, stomps, tiptoes
  Character Traits or what unusual or distinguished features your character has: walking stick, limp, crooked eyebrows, scar

- Tell students that they will be creating a character and writing a description of that character. Explain that the character will need to have human characteristics, but it can be imaginative like Willy Wonka or Dumbledore, or a more realistic human character like James or Charlotte. Students are not permitted to describe a character that another writer or person has already created. (Younger students tend to want to describe a well-known superhero or characters from cartoons or trading cards.) Students will need to also think about whether their character is male or female; they have to think of a name for their character. Remind students that writers often get their ideas from their own experiences and memories, and that they often create characters made up of little pieces of different people that they know.

- Pass out the Visualizing a Character Planning Sheet (see page 110) and provide time for students to record ideas about their characters. Another option would be for the students to draw a detailed and colored picture of their character before they begin to write; this gives them an actual visual to work from.

Lesson 2: Writing

- Return planning sheets and have students share and discuss their character with a partner. Explain that they will be writing a description of their imaginary characters. Remind students that writers often base their characters on people they know.

  Make sure to give your character a name, describe your character in a setting, and give your character an action.

- Model your writing. Emphasize that it is important to not write just a list, but to give lots of details and use similes in a description.

Teacher Model

List description:
Bavis was four feet high. He wore an orange hat and a long green coat. He had black hair and narrow green eyes. He had purple pants and brown boots. He carried a key in his hand and was walking quickly.

Detailed description:
His name was Bavis. He stood only about four feet high. He wore a small orange cap that was tilting to one side and his black hair stuck straight out in all directions under his hat like pieces of liquorice. His narrow green eyes darted back and forth as if he were watching for something to appear suddenly. He wore a long green coat that dragged along the ground when he walked. His pants were purple and puffed at the knees and then tucked into the tops of his brown boots. He held a big black key in his left hand and, as he walked, he waved the key in front of him as if swatting some invisible bee. He looked uneasy as he moved quickly through the wooded path, his green eyes darting from side to side, all the while waving the big, black key in front of him.

Discuss the differences between the two examples. Why is one more visual than the other? Explain that, in the first example, the writer wrote a list. In the second, the writer added details, similes, and examples that really helped paint a picture of the character. Encourage students to write not a list description, but a detailed one.

Lesson 3: Conferencing and Editing

- When students conference with a partner, suggest that they listen to their partner with their eyes closed. Encourage them to make comments on how the partner's writing helped them to visualize. When editing, remind students they can use either the 3, 2, 1…Edit! or 1, 2, 3, 4—Edit! (page 20) checklist to make at least four changes to improve their writing.
- Once the descriptions are written, have students trade their writing with a partner. The partner must read the description and use it to create a drawing of the character.
- Afterward, the students can get together to share and compare their drawings. Partners can comment on what might have been missing in the description— "I didn't know what color his hair was"—providing feedback on where the

Students might be interested to know that often illustrators and authors never meet or discuss how words and pictures might go together. An illustrator takes the words of a writer and uses them to visualize what a character might look like.

writer might need to add more detail. Students can then use their partner's feedback to help them with their editing.

Lesson 4: Publishing and Sharing

See page 86.

Story Strip for Emergent Writers: Visualizing a Character

Name of your character and what he/she looks like	Describe what your character is wearing.	Describe what your character is doing or an action.	Describe your character's personality.

Visualizing an Imaginary Creature

You might follow up Visualizing a Character with another character description; this time, have students create a character that is not human. Students follow the same steps as in the previous lessons to create an imaginary creature. As with the previous lesson, the source for their ideas will be Imagination Pocket, and they are trying to help their readers visualize the creature. See pages 99–101 for lessons.

Anchor Books for Visualizing an Imaginary Creature

Jez Alborough, *Watch Out! Big Bro is Coming* (P)
Lewis Carroll, *Jabberwocky* (I)
Robert Heidbreder, *I Wished for a Unicorn* (P)
Jackie Morris, *Tell Me A Dragon* (P, I)

Il Sung Na, *The Thingamabob* (P)
Ogden Nash, *The Wendigo* (I)
Harve and Margot Zemach, *The Judge* (P, I)

This sample is by a student in Grade 2.

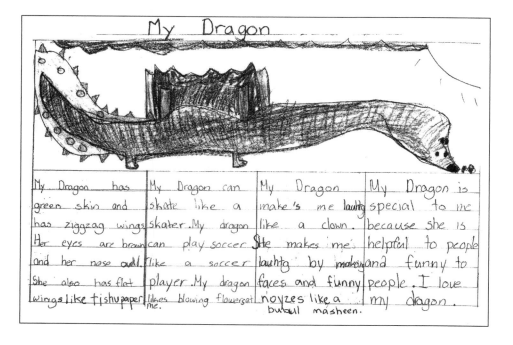

Apple Samples

Sample 1: Apples

Apples grow on trees. Sometimes they are green or red or yellow and sometimes they get brown bruises on them which make them go a bit mushy. Apples can be made into apple pie, apple sauce, apple juice, and apple cider. There are different kinds of apples like Granny Smith and McIntosh. Some apples are sweet and some are kind of sour and not so crispy. Apples are good for you and they say an apple a day keeps the doctor away. They are also good for your teeth because if you forget your toothbrush, apples can kind of brush your teeth for you. If you cut an apple in half you will see some seeds and a core, but don't eat that part.

Sample 2: The Apple

I cup my hands around the sides of the apple and feel the roundness of smooth, cold skin. The flecks of yellow in the redness are like streaks of sunlight. There are tiny flecks of brown and green dancing on one side: the colors of fall. I breathe in the apple—cool, crisp, and fresh. I hesitate to take a bite, not wanting to break the silence of the skin, but I do. I press my teeth into the side of the apple and break open the skin. The crunching sound and sweet taste mix together in my ears and my mouth. I can taste the white flesh mixed with the red skin and they mix about in my mouth, dancing through my teeth and over my tongue. I taste autumn. I look down at the apple and the gaping white hole with teeth marks—an open mouth inside my apple, telling me to take another bite.

Visualizing an Apple Planning Sheet

Name: _____

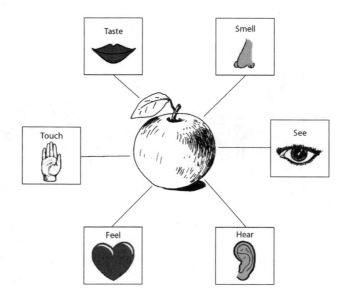

Visualizing Seasons Planning Sheet: Front

Name: _____

Fall is…	Winter is…
Spring is…	Summer is…

Choose one season and one month that you would like to focus on for your piece of writing.

SEASON: _____

Pembroke Publishers ©2011 *Writing Power* by Adrienne Gear ISBN 978-1-55138-263-0

Visualizing Seasons Planning Sheet: Back

Colors	Weather	Activities
_____	_____	_____
_____	_____	_____
_____	_____	_____
_____	_____	_____
_____	_____	_____
_____	_____	_____

Tastes	Sights	Sounds
_____	_____	_____
_____	_____	_____
_____	_____	_____
_____	_____	_____
_____	_____	_____
_____	_____	_____

Smells	Feelings
_____	_____
_____	_____
_____	_____
_____	_____
_____	_____
_____	_____

Visualizing Weather Planning Sheet

Name: _____

Brainstorm as many words as you can for each different type of weather. Try to include colors, feelings, textures, and senses.

Snow	Rain	Wind
Sun	**Fog**	**Clouds**

Now choose one type of weather that you would like to expand into a piece of writing that will invite your readers to visualize. Write your choice here: _____

Complete the chart below with words that describe your weather:

See	Sound	Smell	Taste	Touch	Feeling

Pembroke Publishers ©2011 *Writing Power* by Adrienne Gear ISBN 978-1-55138-263-0

Visualizing My Special Place Planning Sheet

Name: _____

Things I can see:

Feelings I get:

Things I can hear:

People I might see:

A Picture of My Special Place

Things I can taste:

Things I can touch:

Things I can do:

Pembroke Publishers ©2011 *Writing Power* by Adrienne Gear ISBN 978-1-55138-263-0

Visualizing an Imaginary Place Planning Sheet

Name: _____

Things you can see in my _____

(include colors, plants, animals, insects)

_____

_____

_____

_____

_____

_____

_____

Sounds you can hear and smells you can smell in my _____

_____

_____

_____

_____

_____

_____

_____

_____

My imaginary place is a _____

Once, in my _____,

_____

_____

_____

_____

_____

_____

_____

_____

Unusual things that can happen in my _____:

_____

_____

_____

_____

_____

_____

_____

_____

Pembroke Publishers ©2011 *Writing Power* by Adrienne Gear ISBN 978-1-55138-263-0

Visualizing Color Planning Sheet 1

Name: _____

In each color box, list as many things as you can that are that color, including animals, insects, fruits, vegetables, and objects.

Green	Yellow
Blue	**Orange**
Black	**Red**
Purple	**White**

Pembroke Publishers ©2011 *Writing Power* by Adrienne Gear ISBN 978-1-55138-263-0

Visualizing Color Planning Sheet 2

Name: _____

SIGHT	SOUND
SMELL	TASTE
TOUCH	FEEL

Visualizing a Character Planning Sheet

Name: _____

My character is   ☐ Imaginary   ☐ Realistic
My character is   ☐ Male   ☐ Female

My character's name is: _____
Describe your character. Think about…

Physical Traits: what your character looks like; e.g., size, shape, skin, eyes, hair
Personality Traits: how your character acts; e.g., clever, smart, nervous, angry
Character Traits: what unusual or distinguishing feature does your character have; e.g., walking stick, crooked eyebrows
Kinaesthetic Traits: how your character moves; e.g., waddles, limps, stomps, tiptoes

Hair color, length, style	Eyes color, shape	Clothes/Style	Skin

Personality Trait	Character Trait	Kinesthetic Trait	Setting

9 Inviting Readers to Question and Infer

Research shows that good readers ask questions while they read (Pearson, 1983). In my experience, some stories invite readers to question more than others. Walking stories (see page 36), for example, don't invite as many questions because nothing really happens. Climbing stories (see page 36), on the other hand, often invite readers to question *what* is happening, *why* something happened, or *how* a character might be feeling. When a writer tells an interesting and compelling story but intentionally leaves pieces of information out—in a sense, telling without telling—we might ask ourselves *why?* or *what?* or *how?* Once the question has been asked, the invitation is there for readers to find the answer, perhaps forging ahead through the next chapter to find out what happens or why something happened. But other times, a writer might not ever explicitly include all the answers to the questions we may ask. It is the unanswered questions, those unknowns that we encounter while reading, that lead readers to try to figure it out for themselves. This figuring out can also be referred to as an *inference*. Reading causes us to think, for instance, "I wonder why she did that. Maybe…." It is the *maybe*s that engage and deepen a reader's understanding.

For me, questioning and inferring go hand in hand—an inference is a direct result of a question we have no answer for. We infer when there is an unknown: when something is not told to us directly, we naturally shift our thinking into "maybe" mode to try to figure it out. Wordless picture books have become my staple for helping students learn to infer. When there is absolutely no text included, a reader has no choice but to infer what is going on in the story through careful reading of the pictures. For books that invite readers to ask questions and make inferences when reading words, I look for writers who have mastered the technique of writing subtly and not explicitly, telling just enough but leaving just enough out, telling a story by not giving everything away. Readers become more engaged in a text in which the writer has left room for their thinking. It is a gifted writer who can tell a story by not telling the story. There are certain writers who craft their stories subtly, telling just enough but not everything. Writers who want their readers to become engaged in the story weave their *maybe*s through the pages.

In terms of teaching writing, this seems to contradict the writing techniques we've looked at so far; techniques, for example, that encourage students to add lots of details and examples to their writing. However, once students are sitting on the other side of questioning and inferring—the writer's side—they can learn to invite those questions and inferences.

Thinking Power to Question and Infer

Because I see inferences merging out of the questions readers ask, the lessons in this chapter incorporate both strategies together. The first few lessons focus on developing text that invites questions. These are followed by lessons that teach students ways to develop writing that invites readers to infer.

You will notice many writing lessons in this chapter do not follow the structures of the Walking or Climbing Stories that have been practiced in the previous lessons; therefore, story strips for emergent writers are not included for most of the lessons. This is due, in part, to the fact that these writing lessons are based on trying to write a little in order to say a lot; therefore, students are not necessarily following a traditional writing structure. Primary students often use pictures to tell their stories, and several lessons in this chapter include using illustrations or pictures that readers can infer from. Students will be invited to dip into their Memory and Imagination Pockets for these lessons, but with the intent of having all readers dip into their own Brain Pockets to fill in some of the story for themselves.

Lesson: Introducing Writing that Invites Questions and Inferences

- Write this sentence on the board: *Good readers ask questions while they read.* Discuss what a reader might ask questions about (they might be wondering what is going on in the story, why a character did or said something, what's going to happen next, how a character might be feeling, if a problem will be resolved). Ask students where they might find the answers to their questions (in the book or in your head). Explain that, when readers ask questions about a story, it keeps them interested and engaged and they want to keep reading to find the answers. Explain that sometimes a writer might not tell us everything. Ask students why a writer might decide *not* to tell everything, to intentionally leave things out.

  Good writers leave room for their readers to think! If a writer told you absolutely everything, reading might become a little boring. When a writer leaves room for the reader to think, the reader becomes more engaged and interested. When readers add their thinking into a story, try to figure something out, add their own *maybe*s into the text, this is called *inferring*. Inferring is when readers add their own ideas and thoughts into the text. As writers, we want to engage and invite our readers into our stories, and sometimes that means not telling them everything.

- Inferring from a picture exercise: Show students a picture and have them look carefully at the clues in the picture. Have them consider the following:

  What three clues do you think are most important in this picture?
  What are you wondering about this picture?
  What are you inferring this person is feeling? *I'm inferring he/she is feeling _____*
  What are you inferring is happening in this picture? *Maybe…*

  Students can share and compare their thinking with a partner.

Suggested Books for Inferring
Upper Intermediate: Ben Mikaelson, *Touching Spirit Bear*
Intermediate: Frances Thomas, *Mr. Bear and the Bear*
Primary: Anthony Browne, *Willy the Wimp*

- Inferring from text exercise: Explain to students that we are able to infer when we look at pictures by using the clues that we can see, but that we are also able to infer when we read by using the clues that the author writes. Now explain to the students that instead of inferring from a picture, you are going to practice inferring from words. Read the first passage of any story in which a lot of unknowns are presented. Intermediate teachers might choose the first page of a novel where a lot of information is not being detailed.

- Ask the students to think about the following:

  What do they already know? (because the author told them)
  What are they wondering?
  What are they inferring? *Maybe...*

  Have students share their ideas with a partner. After this activity, discuss the following with your class:

  How has this writer invited us in? (because he/she told us some things, but left other things out)
  As writers, what can we try to do to invite our readers to infer? (by not telling everything; by leaving some things out for the reader to think about)

- Explain to the students that sometimes, when a writer is writing a description, it is important for the writer to give the reader a lot of details so that the reader can really visualize and put themselves right into the text. Other times, writers choose not to give it all away because they want to leave room for their readers to think.

  Leaving room for thinking in your writing can sometimes be more difficult than writing it all down. It's almost like trying to write a story by *not* writing the story. When writers leave things out, it's an invitation for the reader to step in.

- End-of-lesson reflection:

  Today we spent some time talking about questioning and inferring. Good readers ask questions when they read. Good readers also know that sometimes a writer doesn't tell everything because he or she wants to leave room for the reader to think. In the next few weeks, we will be learning how leave things out of our writing so that we can invite our readers in.

Lesson: Deep-Thinking Questions

Anchor Books for Deep-Thinking Questions

Tracy Gallup, *A Roomful of Questions* (I)
Tana Hoban, *I Wonder* (P)
Marcus Pfister, *Questions, Questions* (P, I)

Christopher Philips, *The Philosopher's Club* (I)
Louis Rock, *I Wonder Why?* (P, I)
Richard Torrey, *Why?* (P)

- Ask students why people ask questions (to find answers, to learn, to know directions, to figure something out, etc.). Explain that there are two different kinds of questions that people ask.

  One type of question has an answer; for example, What is the capital of Canada? Questions that have answers are called *quick questions* because they are often quick to answer and, once you know the answer, your thinking stops. The other type of question does not have one right answer; for example, Why do I yawn whenever I see someone yawn? These kinds of questions are called *deep-thinking questions* because they invite us to go deeper into our thinking to try to figure out an answer.

When a question has no right or correct answer, it is an invitation to think. It is an opportunity for us to consider our *maybe*s.

- Explain that you have brought in a few books that are all about questions. Most of the questions in the book are deep-thinking because they do not have one correct answer. Read one or two of the anchor books. Choose one or two questions and invite the students to share their *maybe* with a partner.
- Tell students that they are going to have an opportunity to ask a few deep-thinking questions. Make a T-chart with the following headings: Questions About Nature/Questions About Life.
- Model a few questions and then invite students to add their own.

Teacher Model

Questions About Nature	Questions About Life
• Why can't penguins fly? • Why are so many vegetables green? • How long does it take a starfish arm to grow back?	• Why do I yawn when I see other people yawn? • Why are some people mean and others aren't? • Why doesn't it hurt when you cut your nails?

- Pass out the Questions About Nature/Questions About Life sheet, two-sided copies of pages 132 and 133. Invite the students to write and illustrate four questions for each page.

This sample is by a student in Grade 3.

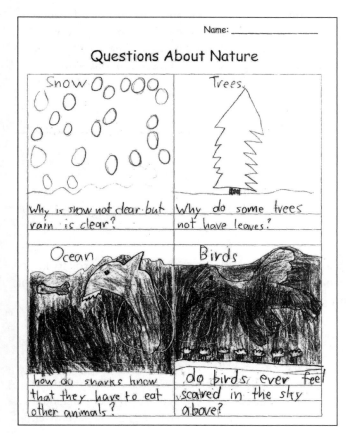

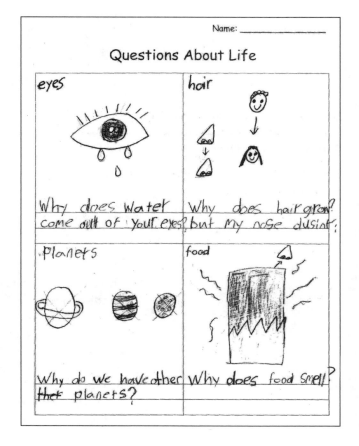

See page 116 for a sample planning sheet.

Students might wish to create mini-books for their questions rather than using blank paper. Fold four small blank pages in half and staple down the spine. Students can record one question and one illustration per page.

Anchor Book: Chris Raschka, *Little Black Crow*

Narrative Power: Walking Story; Poetry

Technical Power: Anchor Lines (p. 47)

Teacher Model

- End-of-lesson reflection:

We ask questions because want to know or learn something. Some questions have answers. Some questions don't often have a right answer. When we don't have an answer, it leads us to think more deeply. Writers who don't tell everything are inviting their readers to add their own thinking into the book.

Inviting Deep Questions

Lesson 1: Planning

- Remind students that you have been sharing books about questions.

When we read a book that is filled with questions, sometimes it invites us to start thinking of our own questions. This book is *Little Black Crow* by Chris Raschka. In this book, the writer is asking a crow a lot of deep-thinking questions. Now, we all know that the crow can't answer the questions, but it invites us, the readers, to start thinking about the answers. It also inspires us to think of questions we might want to ask other birds, animals, or insects—questions they may not be able to answer.

- Tell students that they will be writing a piece that is similar to Chris Raschka's book. Invite students to think about an animal, bird, or insect that they would like to focus on. Then ask them to imagine that the creature can talk, and think about what questions they would like to ask it. Brainstorm a list of things you could ask: questions about family, feelings, friends, food, habitat, abilities, body, interests, likes, dislikes.
- Model your thinking:

Little Green Turtle
How does it feel with that shell on your back? Is it heavy to carry around?
Can you hear things inside your shell? Is it dark in there?
Do you ever get tired of walking so slowly?
Do you ever get lonely inside your shell?

- Have students share the animal or insect they will be writing about with a partner. Pass out the Little _____ Planning Sheet (page 134) and invite students to begin recording their questions.

Lesson 2: Writing

- Remind students that they will be writing a piece that includes a lot of questions.

When writers include questions in their writing, their readers start thinking about questions too. Chris Raschka's book *Little Black Crow* got us all thinking about questions we might ask an animal, bird, or insect.

- Reread *Little Black Crow* and ask the students to notice the writing techniques that Chris Raschka uses. Discuss the use of rhyme and repetition. Explain that they will be using their questions to develop a poem similar to *Little Black Crow*. Explain to students that good writers don't want to confuse their readers, so it's important that they organize their questions into similar topics.

This sample is by a student in Grade 3.

Name: _____

Little ~~striped raccoon~~ Planning Sheet

Choose your animal or insect __raccoon_____

If you could talk to that animal or insect, what questions would you want to ask it? Think about such things as:

Food, family, feelings, habitat, likes, dislikes, nature

Remember: Try to write as if you were talking directly to this animal or insect. Use your voice!

Writer's technique: Repetition!

Start with a few questions here:

1. little raccoon whom do you love?   F.E
2. little raccoon where do you live?   H.
3. little raccoon ~~are~~ you ever afraid of other animals? Es
4. little raccoon where do you go when it gets cold? H
5. little raccoon do you need friends?   F.F
6. little raccoon do you have family just like me? F.F
7. little raccoon does anybody ever protect you from other animals? E
8. ~~little raccoon do your claws ever get sour because~~
   ~~of scurrying around knocking over garbage cans?~~ L.S
9. little raccoon do you ever complain? L.S
10. little raccoon do you ever starve?   F.

Model this organization by suggesting that the students include all questions about family in one section. Younger students might even code their questions before beginning their writing. Remind students about the use of anchor lines or repeating phrases that help to create the rhythm.

- Model your writing:

Teacher Model

Little Green Turtle,
How slow do you go?
Do you ever just want to run and feel the wind?
Do you ever get tired of that shell weighing you down?
Little Green Turtle, are you tired of slow?
Do you just want to GO?

Little Striped Raccoon

Little Striped raccoon, do you need friends?
Do you have family just like me?
Do you have family?
Little striped raccoon do you have a friend to help you though the cold white snow?
Little striped raccoon whom do you love?

Little striped raccoon why do you have fur?
Why not hair like me?
Is fur enough to keep you warm in the cold winters, little striped raccoon?
Are your claws sharp for opening garagecans and getting food without being caught?
Little striped raccoon do your eyes work better at day or night?

Little striped raccoon do you ever feel left out?
Do you ever feel left out?
Do you ever feel proud of yourself deep inside?
Do you ever feel proud?
Little striped raccoon are you ever afraid of other animals?
Are you ever afraid?

Little striped raccoon does anybody protect you from other animals, does anybody ever protect you?
Do you have any enemies little striped raccoon, do you have any enemies?
Little striped raccoon do you ever worry that somebody will attack you?
Do you ever worry?

Little striped raccoon where do you live?
Where do you go when it gets cold?
Where do you go?
Do you have a home little striped raccoon, do you have a home?
Little striped raccoon do you have a home like mine?

The sample above is by the Grade 3 student who chose to ask questions of a raccoon.

Lesson 3: Conferencing and Editing for All Invitations to Question and Infer

Students share their writing in partners and give each other feedback. Encourage partners to infer answers to their questions from the writing. Students then edit their writing for improvement using either 3, 2, 1…Edit! or the 1, 2, 3, 4—Edit! (page 20) checklist. (See Writing Power Conference Record on page 23).

Lesson 4: Publishing and Sharing for All Invitations to Question and Infer

Students may wish to include an illustration with their writing. Invite three or four students to read their writing aloud to the class.

Inferring from Questions

Anchor Books for Inferring from Questions

Barbara Abercrombie, *Charlie Anderson* (P, I)
Anthony Browne, *Willy the Wimp* (upper P, I)
Florence Parry Heide, *Sami and the Times of the Troubles* (upper P, I)
Susan Hughes, *Earth to Audrey* (I)

Frances Thomas, *Mr. Bear and the Bear* (upper P, I)
Chris Van Alsburg, *The Garden of Abdul Gazasi* (or any book by this author) (I)
Margaret Wild, *Fox* (I)

Narrative Power: Climbing Story

Technical Power: First Impressions (p. 51); Dialogue (p. 52)

Read the first page **only** of the anchor books.

Lesson 1: Planning

- Write the following statement on the board: *Good writers don't tell you everything.* Ask students to discuss what the statement means and why an author might leave things out when they are writing (so that the reader becomes more engaged and tries to figure out or infer). Explain that writers leave hints or clues along the way, like a trail of crumbs for the reader to follow. It is then up to the reader to add their own thinking into the story.
- Explain to students that you have examples of writers who don't tell their readers everything. Read through the first page **only** of each anchor book you are using. Explain that the writer did tell us some information, but not all. Ask students to think about some things that they are wondering. Record the questions. Explain that these questions are the starting place for us to begin to infer. Ask students:

  So what do you think is going on here? The writer never actually told us—but what do you think? Share your *maybe* with your partner.

Lesson Two: Writing

- Remind students that good writers don't tell us everything, especially when beginning a story.

  Writers want to give the reader a few very specific things, like a character and a setting and some kind of action, but they want to also leave out few things so that the reader is left wondering. When a reader wonders something, they often infer their own answers, "filling in" what they do not yet know.

- Reread the first page of the anchor books. Discuss the skill the writers showed to start a story by just jumping in. Point out that each first sentence does not explain who the character is:

  This story does not begin with "Once upon a time there was a girl named…" These writers jump in right away with a character in a setting, an action, and often a problem. Right away, the reader knows a little, but is wondering a lot. It's like the writer is saying to their reader "Here—take my hand, jump right into this story with me!"

- Explain that this week's writing will be a short paragraph:

  Make sure your writing will invite your reader to jump into the story, so they can fill in what you did not tell them.

  Post the Jump In! Fill In! chart (page 134) to remind students how writers invite readers to ask questions that they will need to infer the answers to.

Lessons 3 and 4

See page 117.

Inferring Emotions

Lesson 1: Planning

- Remind students that sometimes authors don't tell everything because they want their readers to infer. Inferring happens when a writer leaves room for their reader's thinking. Write *2MI* on the board and ask if anyone knows what it means (a texting abbreviation for "too much information"). Explain that, when a writer gives too much information, there is sometimes no space left for the reader to infer. Ask why writers should not always give too much information away (readers aren't able to infer). Rather than telling explicitly what is happening or how a character might be feeling, the writer leaves hints and clues—the writer does not give 2MI.
- Play a simple inferring game: Have one volunteer be It and leave the room. Show the rest of the class a word describing a feeling. Ask them to go into their Memory Pockets and find a time in their life when they felt this way. Invite the student who is It to return to the class. Choose two or three students to give clues about the feeling. Students can begin a clue with, "I felt this way once when…" The only rule is that students cannot say the actual emotion word when giving the clue. The student who is It must listen to three different clues before trying to infer the emotion.
- After a few rounds of this game, pass out the Inferring Emotions Planning Sheet (page 135). Invite students to think of experiences from their Memory Pockets to help them complete the sheet. If they wish, they can change and replace one of the emotions on the sheet with one of their own.

Lesson 2: Writing

- Return the Inferring Emotions Planning Sheets and have students share their sheets with a partner. Explain that they are going to be choosing one of their feeling moments to expand into a piece of descriptive writing. Review the term *third person* and explain that they will be creating an imaginary character based on themselves, which is often what writers do.
- Suggest students use the "jump in" technique of a great beginning, as they learned in the previous lesson; encourage them to try to include similes in their description. The only thing they must remember is not to write 2MI. In other words, they should not tell the readers how the character is feeling, but instead invite their readers to infer the feeling by leaving descriptive clues.
- Model your writing:

Teacher Model

Feeling Nervous
Memory Pocket: *I felt this way once when I had to sing a solo in front of the whole school during a Christmas concert.*

   Description: *What does nervous looks like? (heavy legs, sweaty palms, heart racing, dry throat, churning stomach, shaking hands)*

   He stood behind the curtain waiting for his cue. His legs felt as if they weighed 50 pounds each. His hands were shaking like a blender on high speed and his throat felt like he had just swallowed sandpaper. The choir was almost finished…the curtains would be opening soon and the fake snow would begin to fall onto the stage. The wool scarf he was wearing felt like it was choking him and his throat began to get tighter and tighter. His stomach flipped over like a pancake as he watched the curtain boy pull the curtains open. It was time…

This planning sample is by a student in Grade 7.

Name: _____

Inferring Emotions
Planning Sheet

disappointed	embarrassed	nervous
I felt that way once when... my best friend did not invite me to her birthday party instead she invited some other boys.	I felt that way once when... I did a careless mistake in my math problem sum when everyone got it right	I felt that way once when... I was about to do a very major exam, Primary School Leaving Examination (PSLE)

✷ stressed ✷	excited	proud
I felt that way once when... School gave so much homework and I had so many supplementry classes and I was so afraid that I would not be able to finish it	I felt that way once when... I was going to get my result slips back for PSLE	I felt that way once when... I've got straight A's on all for subject

After you have completed this sheet, choose one emotion that you would like to expand on in a writing piece.

This writing sample is by a student in Grade 7.

Jennifer was sitting at her study desk in her room, her hair was all messed up and her desk was covered with worksheets and books. She was sweating as she still had not done her homework of 5 pages of math, 5 handouts and study for her Science test tomorrow. The frustrated look on her face. There was a knock on the door, "Honey, are you done? Go to bed." It was Mom. "No! I'm not done! Go away!" Jennifer shouted back. It was twelve in the morning and she's still not done. Her eyes are so tired she could hardly keep them open. "When am I going to finish this?" she mumbled and slams her head on the table.

Lessons 3 and 4

See page 117.

Text Me a Story

Anchor Books for Text Me a Story

Chris Raschka, *Yo! Yes!* (late P, I)   Chris Raschka, *Ring! Yo!* (late P, I)

Narrative Power: Climbing Story

Technical Power: Dialogue (p. 52)

It's a Book by Lane Smith is a humorous look at reading books in the digital age. While there is some controversy surrounding the last line, I like to show students the example of a detailed page from *Treasure Island* being abbreviated into one short text message—it's a great example for this lesson!

For those who may not be up to speed on these abbreviations, there are several websites that include abbreviations and definitions. Just Google "text abbreviations."

You might prepare an anchor chart of text abbreviations for reference or have students help to create one prior to the lesson.

As students develop their own language to communicate through texting, this lesson allows them to use their texting knowledge to create a dialogue that communicates a story but also invites readers to infer.

Lesson 1: Planning

- Remind the students that some writers leave out more words than they actually write, leaving more room for the reader to add their thinking and ideas into the story. If a writer told the reader everything, it could become boring to read because there would be nothing left for the reader to think about. Introduce Chris Raschka as a writer who is able to tell a story by only writing a few words. Share *Yo! Yes!* and ask students to infer what is being discussed by the two characters. Explain that Chris Raschka uses both illustrations and font size to leave clues for his reader to infer. This book has only 18 words, yet we are able to infer the story.
- Write a few "texting" abbreviations on the board: e.g., *lol* (laugh out loud), *bff* (best friends forever), *q4u*,(I have a question for you), *gtg* (got to go). Ask students for the meanings and invite them to add other abbreviations that they know or use. Explain that when we read a text message, often we are left to infer meaning from the codes used.
- Tell students that, for fun, they are going to try to write a story using text messaging abbreviations and punctuation. Remind the class that no swearing or inappropriate abbreviations will be accepted. (This might prove to be quite a challenge to students, so allow them to include some regular words as well). The story will follow the dialogue format of Chris Raschka's book.
- Remind students that a good writer always has a plan before beginning to write. Students will need to come up with
  - two characters (to engage in a conversation)
  - a problem for one character to tell the other
  - a solution for the problem
  Remind students to stick to a very simple problem: e.g., being bored, losing something, forgetting to do homework, being mad at a friend.
- Remind them that this is a climbing story structure; however, they will not be writing a lot of words or explaining the story in a lot of detail, but leaving room for the reader to infer what is happening. Text codes might be included in a "key" so that the reader is not so confused.
- Model your planning:

Teacher Model

Character one: Jared
Character two: Spencer

Problem: Jared is bored.

Solution: Spencer suggests they go skateboarding. Jared is happy.

- Invite students to plan their conversations.

Lesson 2: Writing

- Remind students that good writers sometimes leave room for their readers to infer.

    This week we are using text abbreviations to write a story for our readers to infer.

- Invite students to share their plan with a partner.
- Explain that they will be creating a dialogue (conversation) between their two characters using text messages and a limited number of regular words. Remind them that punctuation can really help readers infer, so to try to include them if possible.
- Give students these guidelines:

    1. Each person can say no more than three words (or texts) per box.
    2. Adding punctuation and illustrations will help add clues for the reader.

- Model your writing:

Teacher Model

Spencer: Sup?	(What's Up?)
Jared: Zzzzz :(	(I'm bored (sigh))
Spencer: GF?	(Where's your girlfriend?)
Jared: lol… RUS?	(Ha! Are you serious?)
Spencer: JK! :) wydg?	(Just kidding. (smile) What are you doing?)
Jared: N/M, u?	(Not much, you?)
Spencer: SK8NG. WAN2?	(I'm going skateboarding. Want to come too?)

- Invite students to see if they can infer the conversation so far. (See translation in parentheses.) Then invite them to help you complete the dialogue. It might not be necessary to complete the dialogue, but doing so will help get the students on the right track.
- After students have completed their dialogues, they can exchange them with a partner and practice inferring.

Lessons 3 and 4

See page 117.

Inferring from Little Text

Anchor Books for Inferring from Little Text

Jez Alborough, *Hug* (P)
Christopher Aslan, *Dude* (I)

David McPhail, *No!* (I)
David Shannon, *No, David!* (P)

Lesson 1: Planning

Narrative Power: Walking Story

- Remind students that writers invite readers to infer by not telling everything. Explain that some writers use illustrations as well as text to tell their stories. Illustrations can help readers to infer because there are often clues you can see in the picture to help you figure out what is going on.
- Share one or two of the anchor books. Explain that each one of these writers uses the same single word throughout the story. Each time the word appears, it means something different. The illustrations often help the reader infer the meaning of the word in each instance.
- Brainstorm a list of words that have been used in the anchor boxes and add more. Not all words will work, but students can try to think of a word that is said a lot but can mean different things: e.g., *yes, no, okay, dude, hug, oh, hey*. Explain that students are going to choose one of these words. They will be writing the one word many times, but each time it has to mean something different. Explain to students that they will have to brainstorm a list of different meanings or situations where that word might be used.
- Model your thinking:

Teacher Model

> YES!
> - I say YES when…
> - I'm excited because our team just won our baseball game
> - I'd like some more pizza
> - I'm here (when teacher is calling role)
> - I'm fine, thank you (if I just fell down)
> - I got the thing that I wanted for my birthday
> - To answer when my dad asks me if I took the garbage out

Students enjoy learning that David Shannon wrote the original *No, David!* book when he was in Grade 1 because those where the only two words he knew how to spell!

- Invite students to add their ideas to your list. Pass out the Inferring from Little Text Planning Sheet (page 136). Invite students to choose a word to use and think of different situations where they might use that word. Explain that if they are having trouble thinking of more than five uses of the word, then they might want to choose a different word. Depending on the grade level, you might set a number of examples for them to use; i.e., four to six examples for Grade 3; eight to ten examples for Grade 6.

Lesson 2: Writing and Illustrating

- Remind students that writers sometime don't use a lot of text to tell their story, but use illustrations to help the reader infer.
- Return the Inferring from Little Text Planning Sheets and invite students to share their ideas with a partner. Because they will be writing only one word on each page, the emphasis will be on their illustrations. Remind them that they do not have to be particularly good artists to be able to show meaning in an illustration.

See page 124 for Teacher Model.

- Model your work. Do a quick sketch on the board and ask students to infer the meaning.
- Invite students to go back to their planning sheets and look over the examples, trying to think of what they would draw for each. There are two options you can provide for the format of this writing: one is a mini-book with several pages, in which students illustrate the word once on each page; or they can use the template on the Inferring from Little Text Planning Sheet (page 136).

Lesson 3: Conferencing and Editing

Since there are so few words, the editing portion of the writing process is not necessary. The illustrations may take a little longer to complete. When students are finished, provide time for them to share their work with a partner and encourage them to infer when reading their partner's illustrations.

Lesson 4: Publishing and Sharing

See page 117.

Inferring a Moral

Anchor Books for Inferring a Moral

Aesop's Fables (P, I)

James Marshall, George and Martha books (I)

Jon Muth, *Zen Shorts* (I)

Jon Muth, *Zen Ties* (I)

Narrative Power: Climbing Story

Technical Power: Dialogue (p. 52)

If you Google *Aesop's fables for kids* you will find many sites where you can access a wide variety of fables.

Lesson 1: Planning

- Ask students why writers don't always tell their readers everything (because they want the reader to figure out some of the things for themselves). Ask the students what a *moral* is (a lesson or a message for the reader). Explain that sometimes a writer will end their story with "And the moral of the story is…" to tell the reader exactly what the message is. Other times a writer does not actually write the moral, but invites the reader to infer what the moral or lesson of the story is.
- Brainstorm a list of morals that the students already know. (You may need to model a few to get students started.) Some may need to be explained. List morals on chart paper or the interactive whiteboard.
- Explain to students that before a writer begins to write he or she knows what moral the story will focus on. Then the writer writes a story where a character learns this lesson through some kind of experience.

- Read aloud one or two of Aesop's fables but do not share the moral. Ask students if they can infer the moral of the story, choosing from the list you created earlier in the lesson.
- After reading the fables, explain to students that the writing focus this week is inferring morals in fables. Explain that a fable is a specific kind of story with specific features:

A fable
- is a short story written to teach the reader a moral or lesson about life
- features animal characters (usually two) who act and talk like humans
- follows a climbing story structure, with a problem–solution format, beginning, middle, and end
- usually includes dialogue (characters speaking to each other)
- often has a first sentence that establishes the character and setting quickly and clearly: e.g., *One day, a hungry fox sat waiting by the roadside.*

- Pass out the Fable Planning Sheet, two-sided copies of pages 137 and 138. Explain that students need to plan their story before writing it. Students can begin to plan their story.

Lesson 2: Writing

- Begin this lesson with a partner share of students' Fable Planning Sheets. Remind students of the features of a fable before they begin to write. Remind them that they should not be writing the moral explicitly anywhere in their piece because the goal is for their reader to be able to infer it.

This sample is by a student in Grade 6.

Once there was a monkey family, which included Mother Monkey and Little Monkey. Mother Monkey told Little Monkey to gather bananas because there was a storm coming. A bunch of his friends were playing soccer. "Hey Little Monkey! You want to play soccer with us?"

"Yeah!" shouted Little Monkey. When the storm came and all of the monkeys went home, Mother Monkey asked him where the bananas were. Little Monkey said he forgot, and they were all starving during the storm.

"Did you learn your lesson, Little Monkey?"

"Yes," said Little Monkey sheepishly. Then they gathered bananas when the storm ended.

Lesson 3: Conferencing and Editing

See page 117.

Lesson 4: Publishing and Sharing

See page 117. Students can type their fables and add an illustration. These can be bound together in a class collection of fables.

Inferring from Poetry

Lesson 1: Planning

Anchor Text: Poem on page 127

Narrative Power: Poetry

Technical Power: Personification (p. 50)

- Remind students that writers sometimes don't give everything away because they want to leave some space for their readers to think. Explain that a poem often has space for a reader to infer meaning because poems are written with fewer words than a story. Fewer words means more room for thinking!
- Write the word *personification* on the board. Review this writing technique: adding the qualities of a *person* (circle this part of the word). Remind students of the three main human qualities: feelings, action, and voice. Explain that they will be writing a poem using the technique of personification. However, they will be writing in such a way that the reader will need to infer what the poem is actually about.
- Invite the students as a class to help you create a personification web by choosing an inanimate object for the topic of a poem. Begin to brainstorm ideas about what that object might look like, say, think, feel, and do if it were human. Invite students to add ideas to the class web:

  Personification: *Hockey Puck*
  Description: *black, round, flat, small*
  Action: *glide, slide, score, flip, hurts, wins games, loose games, causes injury*
  Feelings: *excited, lonely, sore, abused, depressed, conceited*
  Voice: *"Hey! Stop slapping me!"; "I rule this game!; "I am a goalie's worst nightmare!"; "Ha! You missed!"; "Pass me, you fool!"*

- Pass out the Personification Poetry Planning Sheet (see page 139). Explain to students that they need to choose a topic that is inanimate, or not alive. I recommend that students choose either a man-made object—a pencil, a shoe, a coin, an eraser, a fork, a hockey stick, a baseball, a piano—or an object in nature—a star, the ocean, a waterfall, a leaf, a tree, a mountain.

Lesson 2: Writing

- Explain that students will be using the ideas from their planning pages to write a poem.

  One of your goals for writing your poem is to have your reader infer what your poem is about. Because of this, you are NOT to give your poem a title. Also, you have to try to write in such a way as to not give too much information away too quickly. You don't want your reader to figure out the topic immediately, but rather you want to leave room for them to try to infer or figure it out for themselves.

  Explain that students will be writing the poem in first person; i.e., they will be speaking as if they were the object.

- Share the poem on page 127 as a model:

Never-ending torture.
I weigh you down,
Your backpack, your brain,
Your calendar.
I haunt you
and hover just below
the edge of your happiness.
I interfere with your friendships,
Your screen time, your fun.
Just when you think
you are finally rid of me,
I return in a rush of stress,
To fill your mind and your desk.
I hold you hostage all year
And you will only be free of me
At the end of June.

- Invite students to infer what this poem is about (homework).
- Encourage students to play around with ideas and different phrases when writing their poems. Remind them that poems "look" different from writing that has full sentences across the page.
- Older students can attempt to create a more sophisticated personification poem by choosing an issue to personify rather than an object. Examples include bullying, smoking, drugs, gangs, poverty, anorexia, cheating, shoplifting, animal abuse, child poverty, global warming.

Lesson 3: Conferencing and Editing

See page 117. During conferencing, partners are encouraged to give each other advice on what might have been a give-away clue. This might be a line or word that the writer may want to take out or change. On the other hand, a poem might end up being so obscure that the partner might not be able to infer anything, in which case the writer may want to add more clues.

Thank you to Rick Moldowan, who teaches at Silver Creek Elementary School in Salmon Arm, for sharing his inferring poetry with me and for giving me the idea for this lesson.

Lesson 4: Publishing and Sharing

See page 117. Duncan Kay's Grade 7 class at Sexsmith Elementary School created a wonderful display of their poems. The students created a visual (like the one of braces on page 128) and stapled the poem over it to hide it. Passersby would read the poem and then have to flip up the page to reveal the illustration and to check if they had inferred correctly.

Story Strip for Emergent Writers

Primary students are capable of creating an adapted version of the personification poem as a "Who Am I?" A sheet of paper can be folded to show the writing on top and then flip up to reveal the picture underneath.

I am a _____ I am... (Describe what "you" look like)	I can ... (Describe some kind of action that you can do)	I feel .... when... (Describe how you feel when something happens)	"..." (What would you say if you could speak?) Who am I?

Horror,

I tighten,

You see my creator every month,

I make you miserable,

Your pearly white turn silver,

Colourful bands,

I make you feel insecure,

I shift,

Say goodbye to your chewy friends,

I make your mouth bleed,

Excruciating pain,

Silver wires,

I'll be your bully

In middle school,

I live in you,

With you,

When I leave

You better be thankful

Because

You are now beautiful.

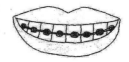

Inferring an Event from Poetry

Anchor Texts for Inferring an Event

Keith Baker, *Little Green* (P)
Shane W. Evans, *Underground* (I)

Valerie Worth, any of her short poems (I)
Ed Young, *Ten Little Mice* (P)

Narrative Power: Poetry

Technical Power: Six Senses (p. 47);
Similes (p. 45)

Lesson 1: Planning

- Remind students that readers are invited to make inferences when writers don't tell them everything. Good writers will leave clues or hints but won't want to give everything away. Explain that you are going to read a poem by a poet who often provides clues for the reader to infer. Read "Fireworks" by Valerie Worth (or any of her small poems) but do not read the title. Have students listen (you may need to read it several times) and invite them to infer what the poem is about. Tell students that Valerie Worth uses many of the writing techniques they have learned, including personification and similes. She also is very skilled at describing something without telling the reader what it is, which is a perfect invitation for her readers to infer.

While some students were able to infer that this poem is about the underground railway, I have heard a variety of inferences, including the rescue of the Chilean miners, a prison escape, an escape from a concentration camp. One student even suggested that the poem was about school!

- Read the poem "Underground" by Shane W. Evans. Do not tell students the title or show them the book. Invite students to spend a few moments trying to infer what the poem is about. Ask them to identify or highlight key words, phrases, or lines that they feel are clues that helped them. Invite students to share their thoughts.
- Discuss the point of view—first person—and the fact that the poem is written in present tense, as if the event is happening right now rather than a long time ago. This allows readers to feel as if they are experiencing the event along with the people in the poem. Tell students that they will be working on developing a poem about an event, but not telling their reader what event they are writing about. The event should be one that most people would know about. It could be a local, national, or international event from the past or present. Spend some time brainstorming ideas with your class. Suggested topics might include holocaust/concentration camp, Vancouver 2010 Olympics, the earthquake/tsunami in Japan, the Stanley Cup riots in Vancouver, the Royal Wedding of Kate and William, climbing Mt. Everest, Terry Fox's Marathon of Hope, the Chilean mine disaster and rescue, devastating tornados or other weather disasters.

This lesson can be an effective way to tie in social studies topics or current events your class may be studying.

- Pass out the Inferring Poetry Planning Sheet (page 140). Invite students to spend some time brainstorming words that they might use in their poem.

Lesson 2: Writing

- Provide time for students to share their planning sheet with a partner. Explain that they are to use the ideas from their planning sheet to create a poem. Remind them that they are not to mention the name of the event anywhere in the poem or give their poem a title. Explain that they are writing in first person, present tense—this means they are to imagine that the event is actually happening while they are writing the poem. They are recording what they see, hear, feel, etc. You may wish to reread "Underground" as an example of present-tense writing. Finally, give a quick reminder that their lines should be short and direct and not be written in full sentences.

This sample was written by a student in Grade 7. It is about the 2011 earthquake and tsunami in Japan.

Rumbling.
Shaking.
A massive shadow.
Sweeping away everything.
We panic,
Scream,
Run.
We're terrified.
It's damaging.
Destroying.
Crashing.
People crying,
Drowning,
Choking,
Missing.
Never-ending horror.
It stops.
Silence.

We come together.
We continue
Hoping,
Wishing,
Living.

Lesson 3: Conferencing and Editing

See page 117.

Lesson 4: Publishing and Sharing

See page 117. Invite a few students to read their poems out loud to the class. These poems could be collated into a class book of poetry. These types of poems could be used to accompany a descriptive paragraph about the event for social studies.

Inferring from Pictures

Wordless Anchor Books for Inferring From Pictures

Tomie de Paola, *Pancakes* (P, I)
Arthur Geisert, any book (P, I)
Barbara Lehmann, *Museum Trip; Rain Storm; The Secret Box; The Red Book* (P, I)
Nikoli Popov, *Why?* (I)
Peggy Ratham, *Good Night, Gorilla* (P)

Beatrice Rodriguez, *The Chicken Thief* (P, I)
Bill Thomson, *Chalk* (P, I)
Sylvia Van Omenn, *The Surprise* (P, I)
David Weisner, *Flotsam* (I)
David Weisner, *Tuesday* (P, I)

Lesson 1: Planning

Narrative Power: Climbing Story

- Begin the lesson:

  Our writing focus these past few weeks has been on inviting our readers to make inferences by not giving everything away. Today I brought in a collection of books to share with you that all have something in common: the writer forgot to write ANYTHING! Imagine—a writer who doesn't even bother to write!

I questioned whether I should include this lesson, since there is no actual writing involved and it has more to do with one's ability to tell a story through pictures. However, in my experience, many children enjoy making comics (particularly boys) so I felt it was worthwhile to include it. Emergent writers use pictures as a means of communicating their ideas and then add more text as they develop, so this lesson will certainly be one that can be adapted for use with younger students.

  Ask students how someone might be able to tell a story without writing a single word (through pictures).
- Share one or two of the anchor books or, if you have enough, pass them out to groups of students to look through. Encourage students to look carefully at all the pictures to find the clues that will help them infer the story.

If you don't have enough books to share, you can choose six to eight pictures from one of the suggested books. Make copies of the pictures and pass out a set to each group. Have students try to organize the pictures in order and infer what the story might be about. Have groups share and compare their ideas about the story before you share the book with the class.

Sherry Devins, literacy support teacher in Salmon Arm, developed this simple and effective way for students to tell a story through pictures.

The final picture can be replaced with any other picture. I recommend providing copies of several different ending options for the students to choose from.

- Discuss the fact that these books tell a story through pictures, similar to a comic book but without any words at all. Explain that students will be creating a picture story. Remind them that, before they began to draw, these writers (illustrators) had a plan of what their story was going to be about, including a character; a beginning, middle, and end; a problem and solution. Encourage students to think about a very simple story line and not to get too complicated. Characters can be people or animals, or both.

Lesson 2: Writing (or Drawing)

- Pass out the Inferring From Pictures Template (page 141). Explain to students that this will be their story grid, similar to a comic strip. Point out that the story already has an ending, but that they are to fill in the beginning and middle. The story has to make sense, of course, and, although students are discouraged from writing accompanying text, they can use transition words such as *first, next, suddenly, meanwhile, finally,* etc.
- Once students have completed their picture stories, invite them to trade with a partner. Each partner can see if they can infer their partner's story by "reading" the pictures.

Lessons 3 and 4

See page 117.

Questions About Nature

Name: _____

Questions About Life

Name: _____

Little _____ Planning Sheet

Name: _____

Choose your animal or insect: _____

If you could talk to this animal or insect, what questions would you want to ask it? Think about such things as food, family, feelings, body, habitat, abilities, likes, dislikes, nature.

Remember: Try to write as if you were talking directly to this animal or insect. Use your voice!

Start with a few questions here:

_____

_____

_____

_____

_____

_____

_____

Jump In! Fill In!

Try to write a short paragraph and

- include an opening sentence that transports your reader directly into the scene of the story

- include a character and a setting. Have your character thinking something, doing something, saying something, or going somewhere.

- perhaps present a problem

- tell SOME things, but not EVERYthing!

- leave out some things so that the reader can INFER!

_____

_____

_____

_____

_____

_____

_____

Pembroke Publishers ©2011 *Writing Power* by Adrienne Gear ISBN 978-1-55138-263-0

Inferring Emotions Planning Sheet

Name: _____

disappointed I felt this way once when… _____ _____ _____ _____ _____ _____ _____	**embarrassed** I felt this way once when… _____ _____ _____ _____ _____ _____ _____	**nervous** I felt this way once when… _____ _____ _____ _____ _____ _____ _____
stressed I felt this way once when… _____ _____ _____ _____ _____ _____ _____	**excited** I felt this way once when… _____ _____ _____ _____ _____ _____ _____	**proud** I felt this way once when… _____ _____ _____ _____ _____ _____ _____

Pembroke Publishers ©2011 *Writing Power* by Adrienne Gear ISBN 978-1-55138-263-0

Inferring from Little Text Planning Sheet

Name: _____

Circle the word that you will be using in your writing:

NO   YES   OH   HEY   OK   DUDE   SWEET   SICK   WHY   HUG

Or choose your own word: _____ (please confirm with teacher)

Now think of different situations when you would be using that word:

I say _____ when _____

I say _____ when _____

I say_____ when _____

I say _____when _____

I say _____ when _____

I say _____ when _____

I say _____ when _____

I say _____ when _____

Fable Planning Sheet: Side 1

Name: _____

A fable is a short story that is meant to illustrate a point or to teach us a lesson or moral. Fables usually feature animals that act and speak like people. Often the moral is not written directly so that the reader is left to INFER.

Step one: Choose a moral from the list on the back of this page. Copy it here:

_____

Step two: Choose your setting: _____

Step three: Choose your animal characters (they should be connected and match the setting):

Animal 1:_____ Animal 2: _____

Step Four: Decide on a problem that one of your animals is having, connected to the moral you have picked.

Problem: _____

_____

_____

Step Five: How will your character learn his/her lesson?

_____

_____

Remember:
- Use dialogue: your characters must say things to each other.
- Start each speaker on a new line.
- You want your reader to INFER the moral, so do not write it in your story.
- Your first sentence should introduce your character in a setting.

Pembroke Publishers ©2011 *Writing Power* by Adrienne Gear ISBN 978-1-55138-263-0

Fable Planning Sheet : Side 2

Treat others as you would like to be treated.

Don't judge a book by its cover.

The early bird catches the worm.

The apple doesn't fall far from the tree.

Beggars can't be choosers.

Slow and steady wins the race.

It is better to be safe than sorry.

What goes around comes around.

An act of kindness is never wasted.

Be careful what you wish for.

Fairweather friends are not worth much.

Don't believe everything you hear.

You are known by the company you keep.

The grass is always greener on the other side.

If at first you don't succeed, try, try again.

Practice makes perfect.

Good things come in small packages.

It is better to act wisely than to appear wise.

Money can't buy happiness.

Work before play.

Beauty is in the eye of the beholder.

Good things come to those who wait.

Look before you leap.

Personification Poetry Planning Sheet

Name: _____

Personification is a writing technique that gives human characteristics—such as action, emotions, and voice—to an object that is not human (an inanimate object). Using this technique, you are going to create a Personification Poem that will invite your reader to infer.

Step 1: Choose an inanimate object: _____
(e.g., a hockey puck, a cactus, a shoelace, homework, a loonie, a mountain, a river, the moon, a pencil, a soccer ball, ballet shoes)

Step 2: Now brainstorm descriptors about your object, thinking of your object as being human.

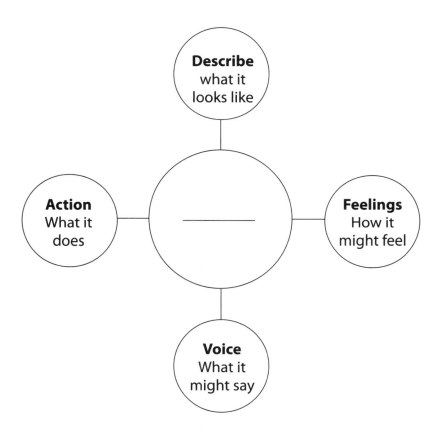

Step 3: Now create a list poem by including your descriptors as clues. Remember: DO NOT include the name of your object. You want your reader to INFER, based on your clues.

Pembroke Publishers ©2011 *Writing Power* by Adrienne Gear ISBN 978-1-55138-263-0

Inferring Poetry Planning Sheet

Name: _____

Topic that I will be writing about is: _____

Sights I see	Sounds I hear
Actions I take (movement)	Smells I smell
Feelings I have	Things I might say or hear others say

Remember that your poem needs to be written in *first person*. Try to imagine that you are experiencing the event as you are writing it. Invite the reader right into your poem!

Pembroke Publishers ©2011 *Writing Power* by Adrienne Gear ISBN 978-1-55138-263-0

Inferring From Pictures Template

Name: _____

Look at the final picture: this is how your story ends. Create a story with pictures to show what happens. You may include only transition words: *first, next, after that, suddenly, meanwhile, soon, finally, at last, after a while.*

1	2	3	4

5	6	7	8
			Meh!

Pembroke Publishers ©2011 *Writing Power* by Adrienne Gear ISBN 978-1-55138-263-0

10   Inviting Readers to Transform Their Thinking

"Think of those times when you've read prose or poetry that is presented in such a way that you have a fleeting sense of being startled by beauty or insight, by a glimpse into someone's soul. All of a sudden everything seems to fit together or at the very least to have some meaning for a moment."—Anne Lamott

One could say that Reading Power evolved out of a bigger question that many were asking of our reading instruction—is this enough? Is it enough to teach children the mechanics of language, the mastery of which results in the ability to decode words on a page? And so now I ask a similar question of writing instruction—is this enough? Is it enough to teach students to write with voice, to organize their thinking, to use a simile to write a description, to use capitals and periods properly? For some, it might be more than enough. But for me there has to be something more. Somehow in our writing instruction we need to make time and space for what really is at the heart of writing—finding and sharing truths.

I tell children that there are all different kinds of books in the world and all different reasons for reading them. Sometimes, when we read a book, we enjoy the illustrations. Sometimes we laugh out loud; sometimes we visualize; sometimes we make connections. Sometimes we read a book because we want to learn about something. But sometimes a book can change the way we think. We read a book and suddenly, or not so suddenly, we begin to think about something differently. We might say to ourselves: "Oh, I had never thought of it that way before." In this respect, books can be transforming, because they can lead our thinking in a different direction.

Most books I have used to support the comprehension strategy of synthesizing or transformed thinking have a message or moral that the author presents. These types of books, I have found, lend themselves most easily to leading children to rethink their position about such things as kindness, forgiveness, taking risks, believing in yourself, peace, homelessness, consumerism. When I teach this strategy to children, I define a transformed thought as a "thinking adjustment" instead of a brand new thought. I also explain that a good reader, even when finished reading a book, does not stop thinking about the book. Often it is the post-thoughts lingering long after the book has been put away that can result in a shift in our thinking. Most important is to teach readers to have openness to this occurrence, to be aware that sometimes a book can change the way we think about ourselves, others, or the world. Once readers come to understand that reading certain texts can change their thinking, they can begin to see the power that their own writing has to do the same for others.

Thinking Power to Transform

When writing these pieces, students will be searching through their Memory and Imagination Pockets to help them find the ideas and the emotions to help them generate their ideas for writing.

Teachers who are now familiar with the story strips will be introducing their students to the *story box* during these lessons. A story box is simply an extended version of the Climbing Story Strip that includes six boxes rather than four or five. Its purpose, however, is the same: to guide students to organize their story. Each lesson provides the guidelines for each box, but generally they focus on the following:

Box 1: Setting
Box 2: Introducing character
Box 3: Adding details, examples
Box 4: Introducing the problem
Box 5: Adding details, examples
Box 6: Solving the problem, ending

Younger writers will add illustrations to each box and will complete their story box by filling in all the boxes. More-able writers using the story box as a framework for developing a longer story will expand each box into a paragraph by adding more details, examples, and dialogue.

Lesson: Introducing Writing that Invites Transformation

- Begin the lesson:

> "An author makes you notice, makes you pay attention, and this is a great gift. My gratitude for good writing is unbounded; I'm grateful for it the way I'm grateful for the ocean. Aren't you?"
> —Anne Lamott

I read a lot of books. Sometimes when I read a book, it makes me laugh, or cry, or visualize, or make connections—or I enjoy the illustrations, or it was a really exciting story. But sometimes, when I read a book, it makes me think differently about something. We sometimes call this a transformation, or a change in our thinking. I like to call it having a thinking adjustment—it's a thought that we already had sitting in our heads, only now the thought looks a little different. Usually when this happens, the writer has passed on something to me—something that the writer cared deeply about and wanted me to care about. Or perhaps it was something that the writer noticed and wanted me to notice. Or perhaps the writer understood something more clearly and wanted me to understand it too. When this happens, I feel a bit smarter, like my thinking just got a little bigger. Writing about things that can change our readers' thinking is a gift we can give them—a gift of thinking. When we write, sometimes, we might actually change the way someone thinks. Isn't that amazing?

Our writing lessons for the next few weeks are going to focus on writing about things in the world that we care about and want others to care about. We are going to pass along a little something to our readers in hope that they might stop and say "Hmmm…I'd never thought of it that way before." We are going to write in hope of inspiring lots of thinking adjustments!

Transforming Thinking About Diversity

Anchor Books for Transforming Thinking About Diversity

Mem Fox, *Whoever You Are* (P)
Sharon Hamanaka, *All the Colors of the Earth* (P, I)
bell hooks, *Skin Again* (I)
Olivier Ka, *My Great Big Mama* (P, I)
Karen Katz, *The Colors of Us* (P)

Shelley Rotner, *Shades of People* (P, I)
Pat Thomas, *The Skin We're In: A First Look at Racism* (P)
Michael Tyler, *The Skin You Live In* (P, I)
Melanie Walsh, *My World, Your World*

Since you won't be able to share all the books in one day, plan to read one each day during the week. If you are also focusing on Transform as your reading strategy, you could incorporate this into your reading lesson by discussing how the book has changed your thinking. You might phrase it this way: "I already knew that… But now I'm thinking…" or "This book has helped me pay more attention to…"

Lesson 1: Planning

Narrative Power: Poetry

Technical Power: Similes (p. 45); Anchor Lines (p. 47)

- Begin the lesson:

Good writers sometimes write about something that can change the way we think about ourselves, others, or the world. Today I brought some books to share with you. All of these books have something in common. Let's see if we can discover what that is.

- Share the titles of some of the anchor books and choose one or two to read. Ask students if they know what the theme of these books might be (cultural diversity; acceptance of others even though they may look and act different from you)
- After reading, explain that, when we read these books, it helps us think about others in a different way. Ask students how these books might change our thinking about others.

Some of us might have already known this, but sometimes reading a book can remind us or help us to understand it in a different way. These books all invite readers to rethink their understanding of accepting others who may look, dress, or speak differently from us.

- Explain that this will be the theme of their writing this week: cultural diversity.

Let's write something today that might help someone else think differently about others. We want to invite our readers to rethink the idea of diversity and acceptance of others, no matter what differences we may have. We want to write something that will make our readers pay attention and say, "Hey—I never thought of it this way before."

- Brainstorm a list of possible differences that we may have from others: physical appearance (eyes, hair, skin, hands, etc.), personality, clothes, homes, food, interests, etc. Pass out the Cultural Diversity Planning Sheet (page 162). Invite students to choose eight differences and record them in the spaces on the left column. In the Me column, they are to describe how they see themselves; in the Other column they are to record information about someone they know.
- You can model a few examples:

Difference	Me	Other
Skin	Peach-colored	Aliya: yellowish with freckles
Nose	Long, with a bump	Mrs. Cottrell: long and straight

This sample is by a student in Grade 3.

Difference	Me	Others
Skin colour	Skin colourbrown	Christopher dark yellow
hair colour	hair colourblack	Ethan blond
Voices	1 language English	Arvin2 Punjabi & English
sizes	Size Medium	Prab tall
homes	Big	Jasmin Medium
clothes	Hockey	Ethan star wars
Style of hair	Straight	Christopher spiky
Hobbies	video games	Christopher pennies

Cultural Diversity Planning Sheet   Name: _____

Lesson 2: Writing

- Remind students that, sometimes, something we write can change the way someone else might think. Remind them that you are writing about accepting others for who they are and not what they look like.
- Return the planning sheets and invite students to share their ideas with a partner. After they have shared, explain that they will be using the ideas from their planning sheets for their piece of writing.
- Introduce or review the writing technique of similes. Model how to begin each line describing differences, but end the line with a similarity that is linked to the topic. Discuss the use of similes and anchor lines throughout.

Teacher Model

See page 146 for a student writing sample.

I am the color of peach fuzz.
My friend Aliya is the color of a speckled banana (including the speckles!)
Our skin might be different on the outside,
but we both get tickles and itches and scratches just the same!

I have a nose with a hook, like a hawk.
Mrs. Cottrell has a straight nose, like a seesaw.
Our noses might look different,
but we both get runny noses when we have a cold!

Lesson 3: Conferencing and Editing for All Invitations to Transform

Remind students when they conference that their partner needs to include "a think"—how reading this has changed their thinking. Use the frame: "I already knew… but now I'm thinking…" (See Writing Power Conference Record on page 23).

Lesson 4: Publishing and Sharing for All Invitations to Transform

Students may wish to include an illustration with their writing. Invite three or four students to read their writing aloud to the class.

> I have black hair like a raven in the sky. But Ethan has brown hair like wheat fields on the praries but we both love jokes.
>
> I speak two languages but Japneet speaks four languages. but we both speak punjabi.
>
> I have dark brown eyes like the soil below but Ethan has light blue eyes like the ocean waters but we both have long eyelashes
>
> I like the Canucks, and dislike Boston and Ella likes puppies and dislikes Brussel sprouts but we both like broccoli.

Story Strip for Emergent Writers: Different and the Same

Invite primary students to use the framework below to write about differences and similarities they share with others. They can try to include similes and voice as their writing techniques:

> I have skin like an apricot. Eric has skin like a chocolate bar. But we both say "ouch" when we get a scratch.

Remind students that the "But we both…" sentence needs to be connected to the topic in the previous sentences.

I have… _____ has… But we both…	I have… _____ has… But we both…	I have… _____ has… But we both…	I have… _____ has… But we both…

Transforming Thinking about Peace, Love, and Family

Lesson 1: Planning

- Write the word *peace* on the board and ask students to think about what the word means to them: what connections they make to it and how it makes them feel. Explain that we all have our own ideas and experiences about a topic and, because we are all different, our ideas and our thoughts can be different. Remind students that writers sometimes write about things that can make us think of something in a different way.
- Read *What Does Peace Feel Like?* by Vladimir Radunsky. After reading the book, tell students:

> I always used to think that peace was the opposite of war, but this book made me think about peace in a whole different way. This book changed my thinking about peace. The book also uses a writing technique that we are all familiar with (the senses).

Explain that this week their goal as writers is to try to write about that topic in a way that will invite their readers to think differently.

"To be a good writer, you not only have to write a great deal but you have to care. You do not have to have a complicated moral philosophy. But a good writer tries, I think, to be part of the solution, to understand a little about life and to pass this on."
—Anne Lamott

Narrative Power: Walking Story or Poetry

Technical Power: Six Senses (p. 47); Adding Details (p. 43); Similes (p. 45); Voice (p. 48)

- Model your thinking. Write the word *home* on the board. Explain that you already know that your readers have a lot of their own ideas about this topic but that you want to invite them to think about it in a new way. Re-create the That's What _____ Feels Like Planning Sheet (page 163) on an overhead or the interactive whiteboard. Invite students to brainstorm ideas while you add them to the chart.

> HOME – brainstorm
> Looks like:
> - *Eating dinner together*
> - *Dad mowing the lawn*
> - *Homework on the kitchen table*
> - *playing cards*
> - *reading together on the couch*
> - *tidy and messy*
>
> Sounds like:
> - *music playing*
> - *coffee grinding*
> - *laughing*
> - *good shouting and bad shouting*
> - *snoring*
> - *"Hurry up, we're going to be late!"*
>
> Smells like:
> - *chocolate chip cookies*
> - *fresh sheets*
> - *cinnamon buns*
> - *sweaty hockey gear*
> - *wet fur*
> - *pancakes and bacon on weekends*
> …

- Pass out the That's What _____ Feels Like Planning Sheet (page 163). Invite students to choose one of the following topics and record it at the top of their sheets:

Kindness
Family
Home
Love
Peace
Friendship

Intermediate teachers might choose to challenge their students by inviting them to choose a feeling to write about instead: e.g., Hope, Despair, Envy, Pride, Fear, Joy, Relief, Gratitude, Excitement.

- Provide time for students to complete their planning sheet.

Lesson 2: Writing

- Return the planning sheets and invite students to share their ideas with a partner. Invite the students to identify two of their favorite ideas from their partner's work.
- Remind the students of the writing techniques that they can include in their writing: Six Senses, Adding Details, Similes, and Voice. Personal details can

make this writing piece very effective. Share and discuss examples of the different forms this piece of writing can be developed: Walking Story with an anchor line or List Poem.

- Model your writing:

Teacher Model

Walking Story Example: *Home*
What does home smell like? Home smells like chocolate chip cookies baking (and sometimes burning) in the kitchen. Home smells like cinnamon buns for my friend Sam (and me too!). Home smells like stinky hockey gear in the basement and Bailey's wet fur after a walk in the rain. That's what home smells like.
(continue with other senses with same anchor line)

List Poem Example: *Home*
Home smells like
Chocolate chip cookies,
Bailey's wet fur,
Stinky hockey gear,
Cinnamon buns for my friend Sam (and one or two for me!)
That's what home smells like.

Lessons 3 and 4

See page 145.

Story Strip for Emergent Writers: What _____ Is Like

Students can choose their topic from the list on page 147.

_____ looks like…	_____ sounds like…	_____ tastes like…	_____ feels like…

Transforming Thinking about Bullying

Anchor Books for Transforming Thinking about Bullying

Derek Munson, *Enemy Pie* (I)
Julia Cook, *Bully B.E.A.N.S.* (P)
Nan Forler, *Bird Child* (I)
Phillip M. Hoose, *Hey, Little Ant!* (P, I)
Mireille Levert, *Eddy Long Pants* (P, I)

Trudy Ludwig, *My Secret Bully* (I)
Peggy Moss, *Say Something* (I)
Phyllis Reynolds Naylor, *King of the Playground* (P)
Alexis O'Neill, *The Recess Queen* (P, I)
Katherine Otoshi, *One* (P, I)

Narrative Power: Climbing Story

Technical Power: Writing in Third Person (p. 49); Adding Details (p. 43)

Lesson 1: Planning

- Remind students that the focus of their writing is to encourage readers to have a thinking adjustment or a transformed thought. Explain that writers often share ideas about something that they care about and that they think are important because they want their readers to care about it too. Share and discuss one or two of the anchor books. Ask students what the books are about (bullying) and why they think the topic is important.

We all know that bullying is wrong but these writers wrote about bullying because they were trying to help us rethink our understanding about bullying.

- Explain that writers often write about something they have experienced before. Ask them to find an experience in their Memory Pocket of being bullied, bullying someone else, or watching someone being bullied. Ask them to share this experience with a partner.
- Discuss what you found in the anchor books:

Why do people bully others? (to feel superior, powerful, controlling, maybe they were once bullied themselves) What does bullying look like? (mean words, teasing, intimidating, threatening) How can you solve a bullying problem? (say "Stop" in *One*; help the bully, in the *Eddy Longpants*; become friends with the bully, in *The Recess Queen*) Why might a writer choose to write about bullying? (to invite us to think about bullying in a different way, to learn some ways to resolve bullying)

- Explain that students will be writing a climbing story about bullying. By this time, the students should be familiar with this term; if not, review the concepts of a Climbing Story, including character, problem, solution, etc. Pass out the Story Box Planning Sheet (see page 164) and set the guidelines for each box.

BULLYING STORY BOX

1. Setting (draw picture)	2. Beginning: Introduce bully (name, description, detail)	3. Problem: Introduce victim (name, description, detail)
4. Interaction: Describe bullying taking place	5. How the problem was resolved.	6. Ending: Describe how things are different now.

- Model your planning:

Teacher Model

1. Setting: school.
2. Roger was a bully. He was rough and tough and liked to pick on little kids.
3. Griffin was small and had short little arms and short fingers.
4. Every day at recess, Roger and his rough, tough friends made fun of Griffin's short arms.
5. One day, Roger's rare Sukiman card fell through a crack between the fence and the storage box. Griffin was the only kid who had arms small enough to get it out.
6. Roger stopped calling Griffin names and bugging him about his short arms. They started trading Sukiman cards together.

- Provide time for students to complete their planning page.

Lesson 2: Writing

- Return the planning pages and have students share their stories with a partner. Remind students that, when their partner is reading, they need to be paying attention to their thinking. Ask: How is your partner's story making you think differently about bullying?

- Depending on the grade level, you may choose to have your students develop their Story Box into a longer piece of writing. Remind students that each box represents one paragraph (or page if you choose to create a mini-book) of the story, but needs to be developed by adding more details, examples, voice, and dialogue. The exception is the setting box, which often does not need its own separate paragraph but can be mentioned somewhere early in the story.

Lessons 3 and 4

See page 145.

Transforming Thinking about Individuality

Anchor Books for Transforming Thinking about Individuality

Eve Bunting, *One Green Apple* (I)
Henry Cole, *Sissy Duckling* (P)
Tomie De Paola, *Oliver Button is a Sissy* (P, I)
Leslie Helakoski, *Woolbur* (P, I)
Olivier Ka, *My Great Big Mama* (P, I)
Cheryl Kilodavis, *My Princess Boy* (P, I)
Munro Leaf, *The Story of Ferdinand* (P, I)
Mireille Levert, *Eddy Long Pants* (P, I)

Leo Lionni, *Frederick* (I)
Patty Lovell, *Stand Tall Molly Lou Melon* (P)
Max Lucado, *If I Only Had a Green Nose* (I)
Todd Parr, *It's OK to be Different* (P)
Dr. Seuss, *The Sneetches* (P, I)
Ashley Spires, *Small Saul* (P, I)
Mary Whitcomb, *Odd Velvet* (P, I)
Charlotte Zolotow, *William's Doll* (P)

Lesson 1: Planning

Narrative Power: Climbing Story

Technical Power: Adding Details (p. 43); Writing in the Third Person (p. 49)

- Remind students that the focus of their writing is to encourage readers to have a thinking adjustment or transformed thought. Explain that writers often share ideas about something that they care about and that they think is important. Writers sometimes want share an important message that they want their readers to think about. Read aloud one or two of the anchor books and ask students to try to notice what they have in common.
- Discuss:

What were the books about? (characters who acted or looked different from others)
What are some of the ways that the writers showed this? (different looking in *My Great Big Mama, Eddy Longpants, The Sneetches*; different interests in *Oliver Button, William's Doll*; different ways of acting in *Woolbur, Ferdinand, Sissy Duckling*)
What was the message of the books? (that what is most important is staying true to yourself, despite what others may think; not changing to be like everyone else)
Why do you think the authors chose to write about this topic? (they might have experienced this; to help us accept differences in others; to help us stay true to who we are)

- Ask students to think about how they might act or look different from others. This could include cultural or religious differences, different interests, differences in appearance, etc.

Have you ever been in a situation where you were not like everyone else? How did you feel? What did you do? Search your Memory Pocket and share your experience with a partner.

- Explain to students that this week their goal is to invite readers to think about individuality, or staying true to oneself. Students can choose to use their own personal experiences from their Memory Pockets or they can use their Imagination Pockets to make something up. They can also choose to have the main character be human (like *Small Saul* or *Oliver Button*) or an animal (such as *Woolbur* and *Ferdinand*). Encourage them to think of an interesting name for their character (such as *Sissy Duckling* or *Eddy Long Pants*). Explain that they will be writing this story in the third person.
- Pass out the Story Box Planning Sheet (page 164). By this time, the students should be familiar with the terms; if not, review character, problem, solution, etc. and set the guidelines for each box.

INDIVIDUALITY STORY BOX

1. Setting: (draw picture)	2. Beginning: Introduce the character and describe how or why they are different	3. Problem: Give an example of how others respond to the character's differences
4. Interaction: Describe some of the daily difficulties this character experiences.	5. How the problem is resolved	6. Ending: Tell how others became more accepting.

- Model your planning:

Teacher Model

1. Setting: pond

2. Fergus the frog was not like other frogs. Frogs are supposed to "ribbet" but Fergus meowed.

3. Fergus was proud of his meow, but his mom and dad were embarrassed and his fellow frogs laughed at him. "Fergus the froggy feline!" they shouted.

4. Fergus had no frog friends but he had lots of cat friends. They didn't seem to mind Fergus's meow one bit. Plus they were furry and warm, not slimy and wet.

5. One day, Fergus noticed a large bird who was about to eat one of his fellow frogs. Fergus opened his mouth wide and shouted "MEOW!" Of course, this scared the bird away and the frog was saved

6. From that day on, nobody minded Fergus the Feline Frog's meowing one bit. In fact, they all decided it was a good way to protect themselves from birds—so Fergus taught them how to meow.

- Provide time for students to complete their planning page.

Lesson 2: Writing

- Return the planning pages and have students share their stories with a partner. Remind students that, when their partner is reading, they need to be paying attention to their thinking. Ask: How is your partner's story making you think differently about staying true to yourself?

- Depending on the grade level, you may choose to have your students develop their story box into a longer piece of writing. Remind students that each box represents one paragraph (or page if they choose to create a mini-book) of their story, but it now needs to be developed by adding more details, examples, voice, and dialogue. The exception is the setting box, which often does not need its own separate paragraph but can be incorporated into the story.

Lessons 3 and 4

See page 145.

Transforming Thinking about Making a Difference

Anchor Books for Transforming Thinking about Making a Difference

Peter Brown, *The Curious Garden* (I)
Barbara Cooney, *Miss Rumphius* (P, I)
Rebecca Doughty, *Some Tips for A Better World and a Happier Life* (I)
B.J. Hennessy, *Because of You* (P)
Anne McGovern, *The Lady in the Box* (I)
Cindy McKinley, *One Smile* (P, I)
David McPhail, *The Teddy Bear* (P, I)
Katie Smith Milway, *One Hen – how one small loan made a big difference* (I)

Emily Pearson, *Ordinary Mary's Extraordinary Deed* (P, I)
Isabel Pin, *When I Grow Up, I Will Win the Nobel Peace Prize* (I)
Christina Reist, *Jack the Bear* (P)
Tom Rath, *How Full is Your Bucket?* (P, I)
Rebecca Upjohn, *Lily and the Paper Man* (P)

Lesson 1: Planning

Narrative Power: Climbing Story

Technical Power: Writing in the Third Person (p. 49); Voice (p. 48); Dialogue (p. 52)

- Remind students that the focus of their writing is to encourage readers to have a thinking adjustment or transformed thought. Explain that writers often share ideas about something that they care about and think is important, and they want to share that with their readers. Writers sometimes share an important message through their story. Read aloud one or two of the anchor books and ask students to try to notice what they have in common.
- Discuss:

What were the books about? (acts that make a difference in the world) What were some of the ways the writers showed making a difference? (helped the environment in *Miss Rumphius*, *The Curious Garden*; helped a homeless person in *The Teddy Bear*, *The Lady in the Box*; did a kind deed for someone in *Ordinary Mary*, *Jack the Bear*) What have these authors invited us to think about? (that even a small act can make a difference; YOU have the power to change the world, even in small ways; don't wait for others to do it—take action) Why do you think the author wanted us to think about that? (they might have experienced someone being kind to them; they believe it's important and wanted us to think about trying to make a difference too.)

- Ask students to think search in their Memory Pockets for something they have done that they felt made a difference in the world. This could include something they did at home, in their neighborhood, at school, at church, by themselves, or with a group. Invite them to share this with a partner. If some children are stuck, invite them to go into their Imagination Pockets and imagine how they might make a difference in the world.
- Explain to students that this week their goal as writers is to invite readers to think about making a difference.

As the writers showed us in the books, making a difference does not have to be something big—it can be something as small as sharing a smile.

Students can use a personal experience for their story or make something up. Have students decide how their character is going to make a difference:

Making a difference to another person. How?
Making a difference to the world (environment). How?

Explain that the story will be written in the third person.
- Pass out the Story Box Planning Sheet (page 164) and set the guidelines for each box. By this time, students should be familiar with the terms; if not, review character, problem, solution, etc. and set the guidelines for each box.

MAKING A DIFFERENCE STORY BOX

1. Setting: (draw picture)	2. Beginning: Introduce the character	3. Problem: Describe what they notice that makes them think about an act
4. Interaction: Describe the act	5. How the problem was resolved: What happened after the character did the act/ deed? What was the reaction?	6. Ending: Describe how the act made a difference

- Model your planning:

Teacher Model

1. Setting: the playground
2. Joy was a joyful girl. Her bedroom was filled with lots and lots of toys, her belly was filled with lots and lots of food, her closet was filled with lots and lots of outfits. Best of all, her house was filled with lots and lots of love.
3. Mia was a sad girl. Her house had no toys, her house had only a little food and even less love. Mia wore the same clothes nearly every day.
4. One day, Mia and Joy were partners in gym. Joy noticed Mia's sad face, old clothes, and skinny legs. At lunch time, Joy gave Mia half her sandwich and her fruity-o snack pack. Mia smiled a thin smile.
5. The next day, Joy asked her mother for two sandwiches and she gave one to Mia. Then she went through her closet and found three things that she had never worn and she gave them to Mia. Mia smiled a big smile.
6. Joy started a "sandwich swap" at her school. Once a week, everyone brought one extra thing to share with someone else. Joy spread joy and Mia helped.

- Provide time for students to complete their planning pages. Remind them to make sure they already know what the deed is and how it will make a difference in the story before they start to write.

Lesson 2: Writing

- Return the planning pages and have students share their stories with a partner. Remind students that, when their partner is reading, they need to be paying attention to their thinking. Ask: How has your partner's story invited you to think about making a difference in the world?
- Depending on the grade level, you may choose to have your students develop their story box into a longer piece of writing. Remind students that each box represents one paragraph (or page if they choose to create a mini-book) of their story, but it now needs to be developed by adding more details, examples, voice, and dialogue. The exception here is the setting box, which often does not need its own separate paragraph but can be mentioned somewhere early in the story.

Lessons 3 and 4

See page 145.

Story Strip for Emergent Writers: You Can Make a Difference!

10 Things I Can Do to Help My World by Melanie Walsh is an excellent model to use for this lesson with younger students.

Younger students can brainstorm things they can do to make a difference in the world.

If I see... I can...	When I... I will try to...	When I... I can...	If I... maybe...

- Model your writing:

Teacher Model

If I see someone littering on the playground, I can pick up the litter and put it in the garbage.
When I see someone who is sad, I will try to cheer them up
When I brush my teeth, I can turn off the water.
If I help my mom, maybe she will feel less stress.

Transforming Thinking about Hope and Gratitude

Anchor Books for Transforming Thinking about Hope

Remy Charlip, *Fortunately* (I)
Maryann Cocca-Leffler, *Rain Bring Frogs* (P)
Michael Foreman, *Fortunately, Unfortunately* (I)

Kevin Henkes, *A Good Day* (P)
Eric Letwin, *Pete the Cat* (P, I)
Leslea Newman, *The Boy Who Cried Fabulous* (P, I)

Lesson 1: Planning

Narrative Power: Walking Story

Technical Power: Anchor Lines (p. 47); Writing in the Third Person (p. 49); Dialogue (p. 52)

The song *"The Sun Will Come Out Tomorrow"* from the musical *Annie* is another good example of a song with a similar message and a repeating line.

- Remind students that you are focusing on writing that invites others to think about something in a different way. Explain that the books you will be sharing all have a common message. Read one or two of the anchor books aloud and ask students to pay attention to their thinking while you read. Ask them to think about what the writer might have wanted us to think about when we read these books. When you finish reading, have students share their ideas in partners.

- Explain that the writers of these books were hoping that reading their books might invite people to rethink how they respond to things in their life. When something goes wrong, we have two choices: to focus on the bad thing or to try to stay positive and not let it bring us down.

- If you are able to, play the song "Don't Worry, Be Happy" by Bobby McFerrin. Ask students to listen to the words and then ask them what the song is about. Write *Don't worry, be happy* on the board. Explain that this song has a message similar to the message in the books (looking on the bright side of life, staying optimistic even when things may seem to be going wrong for you). Point out that the line "don't worry, be happy" is the repeating anchor line throughout the song and one that everyone remembers.

- Ask students to search their Memory Pockets for examples of everyday things that might go wrong and put them in a bad mood (losing a puzzle or Lego piece; not getting a turn when you think you should; not being invited to a birthday party; losing a soccer game; losing something important). Have students share ideas with a partner.

Sometimes, when things go wrong, we focus all our energy on that one bad thing and we forget about all the good things that we do have. Writing about how to turn that energy into something positive can perhaps help your reader think about a bad situation in a different way.

- Make a chart on chart paper or a whiteboard. Model the first example and then invite the class to help you with two or three other examples.

What happened	Negative reaction	Positive reaction
I lost my Lego piece	Get mad Break structure Stop playing Be in a grumpy mood	Find another piece Borrow another piece Feel grateful that I have so much Lego

- Pass out the Don't Worry, Be Happy Planning Sheet (page 165). Invite students to use their Memory Pockets as a source of ideas as they complete the chart. Remind them that they will also need to think of an anchor line. Encourage students to create a catchy anchor line, like "don't worry, be happy" from the song. Perhaps spend a few minutes brainstorming a few ideas together:

"Hey! It's gonna be OK!"
"No worries, mate."
"It's not so bad! Be glad!"
"Cheer up! Stand up and shout 'All right!'"
"Just let it go, Joe"

Lesson 2: Writing

- Return planning sheets and invite students to share their chart and anchor lines with a partner. Explain that they will be using their ideas to write a walking story. Review the elements of a walking story (see page 37). Explain that students are going to turn the examples from their planning sheet into a story that they will write in the third person. The character can be human (like Nate in *Rain Brings Frogs*) or an animal (like Pete in *Pete the Cat)*. The character should show some positive and optimistic qualities so that readers can start to see things in a more positive way. Their repeating anchor line must be included in their story.
- Model your writing:

Teacher Model

Casey Stacy and Joe the Crow were friends, but they didn't always see things in quite the same way.

When Joe the Crow stomped his foot with a grump and a "humph" because he did not get to sleep over at Casey Stacy's house, Casey Stacy said, "Let it go, Joe! At least we got to play together for a few hours."

When Joe the Crow stomped his foot with a grump and a "humph" because he did not get the exact Lego set he wanted for his birthday, Casey Stacey said, "Let it go, Joe. At least you got a new Lego set!"

When Joe the Crow stomped his foot with a grump and a "humph" because he only got a kiddie cone at the mall, Casey Stacy said, "Let it go, Joe! At least you got an ice cream."

When Joe the Crow stomped his foot with a grump and a "humph" because he came in fifth place in the 100 metre dash, Casey Stacy said, "Let it go, Joe! At least you didn't come last!"

- After sharing the sample, ask students to help you write an ending to the story. Explain that sometimes writers actually write the message explicitly, as in this text from *Pete the Cat*:

The moral of the story is no matter what you step in, just keep walking along and singing your song. Because it's all good.

Point out that the writer might leave it up to the reader to infer the message, as in *Rain Brings Frogs*:

Nate says "Behind the clouds, I see sun!"

Lessons 3 and 4

See page 145.

Story Strip for Emergent Writers: Don't Be Mad—Be Glad!

If you… Don't…	When you… Don't…	If you… Don't…	When you… Don't…

Teacher Model

- Model your writing

  If you can't tie your shoe
  Don't give up! Just take a breath and try again!
  When you get a smaller piece than your sister
  Don't complain! Enjoy the piece you have!

Transforming Thinking about Determination and Overcoming Adversity

Anchor Books for Transforming Thinking about Overcoming Adversity

Serge Bloch, *Reach for the Stars: and Other Advice for Life* (I)
Paulette Bourgeois, *Franklin in the Dark* (P)
Peter Catalanotto, *Emily's Art* (I)
Maria Dismondy, *Spaghetti in a Hotdog Bun: Having the Courage* (P, I)
Tom Lichtmindt, *Cloudette* (P, I)
Leo Lionni, *Swimmy* (P, I)
Holly Meade, *If I Never Endeavour Forever* (P, I)

Sebastian Meschenmoser, *Learning to Fly* (P, I)
Watty Piper, *The Little Engine That Could* (P)
Peter H. Reynolds, *Ish* (P, I)
Peter H. Reynolds, *The Dot* (P, I)
Amy Krouse Rosenthal, *The OK Book* (P)
Shaun Tan, *The Red Leaf* (I)
Bernard Waber, *Courage* (P, I)
Mélanie Watt, *Scaredy Squirrel* (P, I)

Lesson 1: Planning

Narrative Power: Climbing Story

Technical Power: Adding Details (p. 43); Writing in the Third Person (p. 49); Dialogue (p. 52)

- Remind students that the focus of their writing is to encourage readers to have a thinking adjustment or transformed thought. Explain that writers often share ideas about something that they care about and they think are important because they want their readers to care too. Share and discuss one or two of the anchor books. Ask students what the books have in common. Ask them what this topic might invite readers to think about differently.

  We all face challenges in our life that we have to overcome. Sometimes we need to find courage and take risks and move out of our comfort zone. Sometimes we need to persevere and keep trying so that we can succeed. Overcoming challenges may be hard, but they make us stronger and allow us to experience things that we may not have ever experienced before.

- Remind students that often writers write about something from their own life experience. Ask them to find in their Memory Pockets the experience of facing a challenge they had to overcome. Examples might include moving to a new school, learning to ride a bike, jumping from a high diving board, trying out for a team or a talent show, speaking or performing in public, meeting new people, learning a new skill such as playing an instrument or a sport. Ask them to share these experiences with a partner.

- Discuss:

What are some feeling words to describe how you feel when you are going to try something new? (scared, frightened, nervous, shy, intimidated) What are some feeling words to describe when you do overcome your fears and take risks? (proud, awesome, determined) What would happen if you never took risks or chances to face challenges? (never know what you're good at, never add new experiences, never learn) What gets in the way of us trying new things? (not believing in ourselves, like Scaredy Squirrel and the Endeavour Bird; others not believing in us, as in *Ish, Emily's Art*) How can we overcome our challenges? (by inner strength/courage, like Cloudette, the Endeavour Bird; by accident, like Scaredy Squirrel; with the help of others as in *Learning to Fly, The Dot*)

Why might a writer choose to write about this topic? What might the writer want the reader to think about? (when you are faced with a challenge, you shouldn't give up, but should try hard to face and overcome it)

You might want to point out to your students that *courage* comes from self; *en-COURAGE-ment* comes from others—but still has the word cour-age in it!

- Explain that this week their goal is for their writing to invite readers to think differently about taking risks, overcoming fears, and persevering. Explain that students will need to create a character who is trying to overcome some kind of adversity, or is trying to take a risk or try something new. Encourage them to think about their own experiences to help them develop the character. Pass out the Overcoming Adversity Planning Sheet (page 166). Provide time for students to complete it. You might model an example.

Lesson 2: Writing

- Remind students that they are writing about facing our fears, having determination, and overcoming adversity. Return the planning pages and have students share with a partner. After they have shared, pass out the Story Box Planning Sheet (page 164) and invite students to use their ideas from their Overcoming Adversity Planning Sheet to create their story box. By this time, students should be familiar with the terms; if not, review character, problem, solution, etc. and set the guidelines for each box.

OVERCOMING ADVERSITY STORY BOX

1. Setting (draw picture)	2. Beginning: Introduce the character and describe his/her challenge	3. Problem: Tell what or who is stopping him/her from overcoming the challenge
4. Interaction: Describe a situation where the character tried but failed.	5. How the problem is resolved: Describe how the character finally overcame the challenge	6. Ending: End by explaining how the character now acts and/or feels

- Model your writing:

Teacher Model

1. Setting: grasslands
2. Jerry the giraffe has a very short neck.
3. He can't reach the juicy leaves from the tops of the trees and gets only the small dry ones.
4. He tries climbing a tree but he falls.
5. One day, he is eating the dry leaves at the bottom of a rubber tree plant and gets some sticky rubber on the bottom of his feet. He stomps up and down to get the sticky rubber off and discovers he can jump very high.
6. Now Jerry can reach the leaves by jumping up high into the trees.

- Proficient writers who complete their story boxes quickly can develop their story boxes into a more substantial story by adding more details, examples, voice, and dialogue. The exception here is the setting box, which often does not need its own separate paragraph.

Lessons 3 and 4

See page 145

Transforming Thinking about What Is Most Important

Anchor Books for Transforming Thinking about What Is Important

Jutta Baur, *Selma* (I)
Byrd Baylor, *The Table Where Rich People Sit* (I)
Maribeth Boelts, *Those Shoes* (I)
Greg Foley, *Willoughby and the Lion* (P, I)
Nan Gregory, *Pink* (I)
Linda Kranz, *Only One You* (P)

Colin McDougall, *The Gift of Nothing* (P, I)
Jon Muth, *The Three Questions* (I)
Colin Thompson, *The Short and Incredible Happy Life of Riley* (I)
Colin Thompson, *The Big Little Book of Happy Sadness* (I)

Lesson 1: Planning

Narrative Power: Climbing Story

Technical Power: Similes (p. 45); Adding Details (p. 43); Writing in Third Person (p. 49); Dialogue (p. 52)

- Ask students if they have ever wished for something that they didn't have but wanted (special toy, brand-name shoes, a cell phone, an iPad, a trip somewhere, a rare trading card, a special type of clothing). Have them share with a partner. Ask them to describe how they feel when they see others who have this item when they don't. Share one or two of the anchor books and discuss what students think might be the common message. Ask what the writers of these books might have wanted us to think or rethink about (that money, fancy houses, and lots of stuff might appear to be what is most important, but really, what is most important is that we are with people we care about, that we feel love and give love). Also point out that the books might invite readers to think about being grateful for all the things they do have, instead of wishing for the things they don't have.
- Discuss:

What do you think is the most important thing or the secret of happiness? Why do people always seem to want more stuff but often don't seem happy? In many of the suggested anchor books, a question is being asked. How do these questions invite readers to think?

Nicholi (*The Three Questions*) is wondering how to be a good person. Mooch (*Gift of Nothing*) is wondering what gift to get his friend who already has everything. The dog (*Selma*) is wondering what happiness is. Willoughby (*Willoughby and the Lion*) is wondering what to wish for. People (*The Short and Incredibly Happy Life of Riley*) want to know how to live forever and be happy and healthy.

How do we discover answers to these deep life questions? (through self discovery, through experiences, with the help of someone else)

- Explain that students will be writing a piece about a character who is searching for an answer to a big question.
- Brainstorm a list of possible big questions:

  What is happiness?
  What is the most important thing?
  Why are we here?
  What is the meaning of life?

- Pass out What's Most Important Planning Sheet (page 167). Remind students that they will be writing in third person and that they need to develop a character who is searching for an answer to a big question. Students might wish to plan their story with a partner.

Lesson 2: Writing

- After the students have completed their planning sheet, they can begin to organize their story into a Story Box grid.

WHAT IS MOST IMPORTANT STORY BOX

1. Setting:	2. Beginning: Introduce your character and tell a little about him or her	3. Problem: Explain what big question your character is searching to answer (make sure your question has something to do with searching for happiness or what's most important)
4. Interaction: Describe how your character searches for the answer to the "big question" but doesn't find the answer	5. How the problem is resolved: Describe how the character eventually finds the answer	6. Ending: How has the answer changed the character?

- Students can use the Story Box Grid (see page 164) as they begin to write their story. Once the boxes are complete, older students may want to expand each of the boxes into a more detailed paragraph in order to develop a longer writing piece.

- Model your writing:

William liked stuff. The more stuff he got, the more he wanted. The problem was, he didn't really spend time using the stuff.

One day, his mother asked "Don't you have enough stuff?" William said "Never—I will never have enough stuff!"

But soon, he began to wonder, "How much is enough stuff?"

William asked his friend, Simran, "How much is enough stuff?"

Simran replied, "I don't think there's EVER enough stuff!"

William asked his grandma, "How much is enough stuff?" His grandma answered, "That depends on what you call stuff. Is stuff something you can hold or something you can feel?"

William didn't know.

- Ask the class to help you with an ending: How can William learn that getting more and more stuff is not really going to make him happy?

Lessons 3 and 4

See page 145.

Cultural Diversity Planning Sheet

Name: _____

Differences can include likes, dislikes, appearance, hobbies, interests, homes, culture, talents

Differences	Me	Other (name)

That's What _____ Feels Like Planning Sheet

Name: _____

Looks like…	Sounds like…

Smells like…	Tastes like…

Feels like (touch)…	Feels like (emotion)…

Story Box Planning Sheet

Name: _____

1. Setting:	2. Beginning:	3. Problem:
	_____	_____
	_____	_____
	_____	_____
	_____	_____
	_____	_____
	_____	_____
	_____	_____
	_____	_____
	_____	_____
	_____	_____
	_____	_____
	_____	_____
4. Interaction:	5. How the problem is resolved:	6. Ending:
_____	_____	_____
_____	_____	_____
_____	_____	_____
_____	_____	_____
_____	_____	_____
_____	_____	_____
_____	_____	_____
_____	_____	_____
_____	_____	_____
_____	_____	_____

Pembroke Publishers ©2011 *Writing Power* by Adrienne Gear ISBN 978-1-55138-263-0

Don't Worry, Be Happy Planning Sheet

Name: _____

What Happened	Negative Reaction	Positive Reaction

Anchor Line: _____

Pembroke Publishers ©2011 *Writing Power* by Adrienne Gear ISBN 978-1-55138-263-0

Overcoming Adversity Planning Sheet

Name: _____

Main Character Choose one: ☐ Human character ☐ Animal character Name: _____	Draw a picture of this character
What challenge does this character face? Choose one: ☐ Personal fear ☐ Something getting in their way ☐ Someone getting in their way	Explain: _____'s challenge is that he/she _____ _____ _____ _____ _____
How does your character overcome his/her challenge? Choose one: ☐ By their own courage or perseverance ☐ By the help of someone else ☐ By accident	Explain: _____ overcomes his/her challenge _____ _____ _____ _____ _____

What's Most Important? Planning Sheet

Name: _____

Main Character Choose one: ☐ Human character ☐ Animal character Name: _____	Draw a picture of this character
What question about life will your character be asking and searching for the answer to? _____ _____ _____ _____ _____ _____ _____	What is the answer that you want the reader to think about? _____ _____ _____ _____ _____ _____ _____
How will the character come find the answer to his/her question? Choose one: ☐ By their own discovery ☐ Accidently ☐ With the help of someone else	Explain: _____ _____ _____ _____ _____ _____

Pembroke Publishers ©2011 *Writing Power* by Adrienne Gear ISBN 978-1-55138-263-0

Final Thoughts

"If you are teaching and not learning, you are not teaching."
—Frank McCourt

As teachers, we are on a continual learning journey, searching for new ways to help our students reach their greatest potential. Finding myself on the giving end of a book for teachers, I feel a huge amount of pressure, for I know that many on the receiving end of this book bring to it a wealth and depth of expertise and knowledge about writing instruction, having journeyed far down the learning path, while others may be just at the beginning of this amazing journey I call teaching. My dear friend and colleague, Amy Wou, said it best when she said that every once in a while teachers need "an injection of something inspiring"—I hope this book has done just that. For all of you, I wish to say how much I hope this book brings you practical ideas for teaching your students to write with a greater awareness of how to engage their readers through their ideas and words. I hope, as well, that this book will provide for you a space to perhaps rethink what it means to write; to share ideas and thoughts with others; to "gift" someone with your words. If I have helped you in some small way along your learning journey, it has been my privilege.

Acknowledgments

In this book, I speak of "the gift of words" shared between reader and writer. I also consider people to be gifts and I am blessed to have an abundant supply of them.

It has become a longstanding joke among those who actually read the acknowledgment pages of a book that mine are the longest they have ever seen. Try as I might, I cannot bring myself to simplify my gratitude into a few initials—"A.G. would like to thank R.G." So, bear with me as I once again acknowledge with thanks a long list of people without whom this book could not have been written.

First, I would like to express my gratitude to the extraordinary group of teachers at J.W. Sexsmith Elementary School in Vancouver, with whom I have had the privilege of working for the past three years. Although I am only there part-time, I feel at home in that school. Many of the teachers willingly and graciously allowed me into their classrooms to try out these writing lessons with their students. In particular, my thanks to Duncan Kay, Julie Mason, Michelle Sprintzios, Kelly Cooksley, Jeannette Owen, Mari Matsuo, Leslie Wolrich, Margo McGarry, Sarah Shankland, Wendy Hugli, Carole Murray, and Kimberly Matterson. Thanks to Jacquie Hall, school administrator, for supporting my work both inside and outside the school. A special thank you to Mary Cottrell and Jeanette Mumford, who not only invite me into their rooms, rearrange their timetables for me, cancel their preps so they can listen to the lessons, correct my spelling, and give me feedback and suggestions, but also remind me every time I visit their classrooms what it feels like to make a difference. Thanks to the extraordinary students of Sexsmith Elementary (I'd name them all but my publisher won't let me) who have taught me, through their writing, that words are indeed a gift from one to another. They have "gifted" me time and time again and I will be forever grateful.

When I'm not teaching students, I have the fortunate position to be working with amazing educators around the province. I have been welcomed into districts, schools, and classrooms, and I am grateful to have been given the opportunity to share ideas and witness the passion and dedication of so many outstanding teachers, administrators, teacher-librarians, support staff, and district staff who strive every day to make learning better for children. While too many to name, I would like to acknowledge with gratitude the following: Kathy Eades and the teachers of SD 82 (Terrace); Wendy Woodhurst, Sherry Devins, and the teachers of SD 83 (North-Okanagan/Shuswap); Bev Young and the teachers of SD 54 (Smithers); Kristi Johnston, Heather Rapin, Mary Philpot, and the teachers of SD 75 (Mission); Ngaire Leaf and the teachers of SD 35 (Langley); Nancy Carle and the teachers of SD 43 (Coquitlam); Cheryl Burian, Laura Birarda, Janice Novakowski, Tedd Lim, and the teachers of SD 38 (Richmond); Tanis Carter, Christy Northway, Norene Campion, Monica Arora, Laura Grills, Krista Forbes, and the teachers of SD 36 (Surrey); Judi Mathot and the teachers of SD 42 (Burnaby); Sandra Huggett and the teachers of SD 57 (Prince George); Nancy Gordon, Catherine Watson, and the teachers of SD 37 (Delta); Drew Williams, Melodie Beatty, Mary Kretlow, Ruth Kline, and the teachers of SD 72 (Campbell River); Maria Limpright, Rob Carmichael, Edward Bradford, and the teachers of SD 34 (Abbotsford); Tandy Gunn and the teachers of SD 69 (Parksville); Deanna Steptoe, Katie McCormack, and the teachers of SD 73 (Kamloops); Carole Johns and the teachers of SD 20 (Cranbrook); Val Collins, Jeanette McCrie, and the teachers in Whitehorse SD; Lori Harris, Mandy Richmond, Ian Kennedy, and the teachers of Collingwood Jr. and Sr. School (West Vancouver); Stella Arujo, Stephanie Horvath, Susan Van Blarcom, and the teachers of Crofton House Elementary School (Vancouver); Selina Mui and the teachers of West Point Grey Academy (Vancouver); Gordon Macintyre and the teachers of Stratford Hall Jr. School (Vancouver); Kathy Kealey, Karen Webb, and the teachers of York House Jr. School (Vancouver).

It is a challenge to try to write a book when there is this little thing called life that requires your attention. Thankfully, I have had the gentle (and sometimes not so gentle) push, sideline cheering, and unconditional support from a number of dear friends. Thank you to Cheryl Burian, Sue Stevenson, Kimberly Matterson, Donna Boardman, Katie McCormack, Amy Wou, and Carrie Gleason who, in their own time and own way, helped me complete this book. Always an extra special thank-you to my dear Cheryl who, upon request, made regular "Get writing!" phone calls and "Shouldn't you be writing?" e-mails that helped me forge ahead to the finish line. I also could not have managed to complete this project without the support of my two sisters, Alison Gear and Janet Gear. I am grateful to you both for your words of wisdom and encouragement that helped me through many moments of doubt.

I am grateful to the editing advice and helpful suggestions from Laura Grills, Cheryl Burian, and Krista Forbes. Special thanks to Linda O'Reilly for her generous wisdom and insight, and for asking the big questions. Thank you to Meredyth Kezar for her enthusiastic support of my debut Writing Power workshop and for her continued friendship.

Thanks to my book-club friends who, for many years, have listened politely while I shared my connections, visual images, inferences, and questions, and who are now putting up with my comments on writing techniques. I am grateful to have a place to share my thinking about the books I read with such wonderful women. Thank you to Cheryl, Heather, Anna, Bonnie, Stella, Laura B, Laura G, Krista, Melanie, Jarma, and Maria.

To Phyllis Simon, Maggie de Vries, Susan McGuigan, James McCann, Sarah Bagshaw, and the amazing staff at all three Kidsbooks stores—thank you for supporting teachers, students, and parents across the province by providing them with a place in their community where they can be surrounded by lovely books and lovely people. It is Christmas every day in your store. Thank you to Nadia Fortuna and Elizabeth Graves at United Library Services for their amazing support and efforts in supplying teachers with easy access to recommended Reading Power books, and for welcoming me into their warehouse with a coffee and an empty shopping cart to fill. I can't think of a better way to spend a morning. Thank you to Doreen Metcalfe and the amazing staff at School House Teaching Supplies and Children's Bookstore in Victoria for their support of Reading Power and their tireless efforts in supplying outstanding children's books to teachers and students all across Vancouver Island.

I am enormously grateful to Mary Macchiusi, the publisher at Pembroke, for her patience and encouragement—and for not giving me a deadline until I asked for one. To Kat, my amazing editor: I am grateful for her guidance and her extraordinary ability to shape my sometimes scattered pieces of thinking into a cohesive whole.

Finally, to the three most important people in my life: Richard, my dear husband, who has quietly and selflessly filled in the many gaps left behind by the writing of this book, particularly during the final stretch. It is not easy to be married to me and I could not be doing what I do without him. And to my two boys, Spencer and Oliver: no words can ever describe how grateful I am to be your mum. You have filled every corner of my Memory Pocket with joy. I am abundantly grateful to have not only a job that fuels my thinking, but also a family that fuels my heart.

Professional Resources

Arter, Judith; Spandel, Vicki; Culham, Ruth; & Pollard, Jim (1994) *The Impact of Training Students to be Self-Assessors of Writing*. Paper presented at AERA in New Orleans, LA.

Atwell, N. (1998) *In the Middle: new understandings about writing, reading and learning* (2nd ed). Portsmouth, NH: Heinemann.

Atwell, N. (2002) *Lessons That Change Writers*. Portsmouth, NH: Heinemann

BC Ministry of Education (2006) *English Language Arts Grades K–7 IRP*. also available online at: bced.gov.bc.ca

Bellamy, P. (2002) *Research on Writing with the 6+1 Traits*. The Northwest Regional Educational Laboratory.

Bellamy, P. (2004) *Picture Books: an annotated bibliography with activities for teaching writing with the 6+1 Trait Writing model*. Portland, OR: NWREL.

Buckner, A. (2005) *Notebook Knowhow: Strategies for the writer's notebook*. Portland, ME: Stenhouse.

Calkins, L.M. (1994) *The Art of Teaching Writing*. Portsmouth, NH: Heinemann.

Culham, R. (2003) *6+1 Traits of Writing: the complete guide grade 3 and up*. New York NY: Scholastic.

Culham, R. (2004) *Using Picture Books to Teach Writing with the Traits*. New York, NY: Scholastic.

Culham, R. (2005) *6+1 Traits of Writing: the complete guide for primary grades*. New York, NY: Scholastic.

Diederich, P.B.; French, J. W.; & Carlton, S.T. (1961) *Factors in the Judgment of Writing Quality*. Princeton, NJ: Educational Testing Service.

Diederich, P.B. (1974) *Measuring Growth in English*. Urbana, IL: NCTE.

Donohue, L. (2009) *The Write Beginning*. Markham, ON: Pembroke.

Dorfman, L.R. & Cappelli, R. (2007) *Mentor Texts: Teaching writing through children's literature K–6*. Portland, ME: Stenhouse.

Ellis, S. (2000) *From Reader to Writer: teaching writing through classic children's books*. Toronto, ON: Groundwood Books.

Fletcher, R. & Portalupi, J. (2001) *Writing Workshop: The essential guide*. Portsmouth, NH: Heinemann

Fletcher, R. & Portalupi, J. (1998) *Craft Lessons: teaching writing K–8* (2nd ed). Portland, NH: Stenhouse.

Fletcher, R. (1992) *What a Writer Needs*. Portsmouth, NH: Heinemann.

Fletcher, R. (1999) *Live Writing: Breathing life into your words*. New York, NY: Harper Collins.

French, P.B. & Carlton, S.T. (1961) *Factors in the Judgment of Writing Quality*. Princeton, NJ: Educational Testing Service.

Gash, A. (2004) *What the Dormouse Said: Lessons for grown-ups from children's books*. Chapel Hill, NC: Algonquin Books.

Gear, A. (2006) *Reading Power: teaching students how to think while they read.* Markham, ON: Pembroke.

Glover, M. (2009) *Engaging Young Writers K–1.* Portsmouth, NH. Heinemann.

Graves, D.H. (1975) "An examination of the writing processes of seven-year-old children" *Research in the Teaching of English,* 9, 227–41.

Graves, D.H. (1983) *Writing: Teachers and children at work.* Portsmouth, NH: Heinemann.

Graves, D. & Hansen, J. (1983) "The Author's Chair" *Language Arts,* 60 (2), 176–83.

Green, J. (2010) *How Bullets Saved My Life: fun ways to teach some serious writing skills.* Markham, ON: Pembroke.

Harvey, S. & Goudvis, A. (2007) *Strategies That Work: Teaching comprehension to enhance understanding* (2nd ed). Portland, ME: Stenhouse.

Harwayne, S. (1992) *Lasting Impressions: Weaving literature into the writing workshop.* Portsmouth, NH: Heinemann.

Harwayne, S. & Calkins, L. (1990) *Living Between the Lines.* Portsmouth, NH: Heinemann.

Heard, G. (1999) *Awakening the Heart: Exploring poetry in elementary and middle school.* Portsmouth, NH: Heinemann.

Johnson, K. & Westcott, P. (2004) *Writing Like Writers: Guiding elementary children through a writer's workshop.* Austin, TX: Prufrock Press.

Lamott, A. (1995) *Bird by Bird: Some instructions on writing and life.* New York, NY: Anchor Books.

Murray, D.M. (2003) *A Writer Teaches Writing* (Revised 2nd ed). Belmont, CA: Wadsworth Publishing.

North Vancouver School District (2007) *Writing 44 Intermediate: a core writing framework.* Victoria, BC: Queen's Printer.

North Vancouver School District (2009) *Writing 44 Primary: a core writing framework.* Victoria, BC: Queen's Printer.

Pearson, D. & Gallagher, M. (1983) "The Instruction of Reading Comprehension" *Contemporary Educational Psychology* 8: 317–344.

Reid, J. & Schultze, B. (2005) *What's Next for this Beginning Writer.* Markham, ON: Pembroke.

Rog, L.J. (2010) *Marvellous Mini Lessons for Teaching Intermediate Writing, Grades 4–6.* Newark, DE: International Reading Association.

Rog, L.J. (2007) *Marvellous Mini Lessons for Teaching Beginning Writing K–3.* Newark, DE: International Reading Association.

Routman, R. (2004) *Writing Essentials: Raising expectations and results while simplifying teaching.* Portsmouth, NH: Heinemann.

Spandel, V. & Stiggins, R. (1990) *Creating Writers: Linking assessment with writing instruction.* New York, NY: Longman.

Spandel, V. (2005) *Creating Writers Through the 6-Trait Writing Assessment and Instruction* (4th ed). Boston, MA: Pearson Educational Inc.

Spandel, V. & Hicks, J. (2003) *The Write Traits.* Wilmington, MA: Great Source (Houghton Mifflin Harcourt).

Wells, J. & Reid, J. (2004) *Writing Anchors.* Markham, ON: Pembroke.

Index